NEUROSCIENCE OF INCLUSION

New Skills for New Times

MARY E. CASEY & SHANNON MURPHY ROBINSON

outskirts
press

To Tim and Emily, my amazing siblings, and all the incredible friends who have supported me in my journey to wholeness. It is because of all of you that it's even possible for me to write this book.

To Annabelle - thank you for being my inspiration to delve deeply into neuroscience. To Gerald, Gabrielle and Rachael - thank you for your love and support on this journey of our lives. I'm so lucky to have all of you in my life.

Table of Contents

Acknowledgements

We would like to express our gratitude to the many people who supported us throughout the writing of this book. We would like to thank Dr.
Srini Pillay, MD, Harvard Professor and CEO of the NeuroBusiness Group
for providing a challenging and thorough Advanced Certification in the
neuroscience of leadership coaching. A very special thanks also goes to
Dr. William B. Hosfield, MD, and friend for his on-going encouragement
and invaluable feedback as we worked to translate neuroscience findings
into lay terms, and for observing our presentations to further help us
apply neuroscience findings to inclusion. To Karen Stinson, founder and
former CEO of the global diversity and inclusion consultancy ProGroup,
for reading our early drafts and providing invaluable insight and feedback, and for her guidance, wisdom and creativity as our business mentor
and coach. To our early client supporters – Seagate, Hennepin County,
Be the Match, St. Catherine University, the Association of Certified Trial
Lawyers, the Society for Intercultural Education, Training and Research
(SIETAR), and the Twin Cities Diversity Roundtable – for believing in us
and inviting us to present our brain-based inclusion training programs
before we had a solid track record in this new approach. A very special
thanks also goes to our colleague, diversity and inclusion consultant Tony
Orange, for his ongoing encouragement and the hours he freely gave
helping us strengthen and refine our content. Thank you to Lisa Griebel

for her expertise and valuable input as we created our BrainStates Management™ Certification Program. To Amy Perez Ortiz and Steven Humerickhouse at the Forum on Workplace Inclusion for supporting our work when no one was talking about neuroscience, and for their ongoing support throughout our many presentations at the Forum.

We thank everyone who has helped in the final push to complete this book. Thank you to Marsha Wagner at CastleVisions for your great work editing our book, and Mike Steinkamp at Great Rate Graphics for all your help creating the graphics. Special thanks and appreciation goes to Tina Ruvalcaba, our publishing consultant, and Brittney, our author representative, at Outskirts Press for helping us with all the moving parts in the journey to get the book published.

Above all we want to thank our families. To our husbands – Tim Jordheim and Gerald Robinson – for their unwavering support, and without whom this book would never have found its way to completion. We cannot express the depth of our gratitude to each of you for your ongoing encouragement and steadfast humor through all the re-writes, set-backs, and often long weekend hours we spent bent over our computers. To our girls – Emily Jordheim, Gabrielle Robinson, Rachael Robinson, and Annabelle Robinson – we say thank you from the bottom of our hearts for your patience and understanding, and for your curiosity, thoughtful questions and incredible insights on what it really means to be inclusive. You are the reason this book matters, for it is in your lifetimes that inclusion will have its opportunity to thrive.

Introduction

"The universe is wider than our views of it."
        - Henry David Thoreau

We stand at the beginning of a new era. Through advanced imaging technologies such as magnetic resonance imaging (MRI) and the functional MRI (fMRI), it is now possible to study the brain in real time. For the first time in history, we have specific information about the brain's underlying circuitry, functions, and processes, and how these directly influence our experiences, perceptions, and beliefs - all under the radar of our conscious awareness. This unprecedented window into the inner working of the brain also has immediate relevancy for advancing diversity and inclusion skills in the workplace. From neuroscience, we now have significant new information and insight into how biases operate in the brain, what we can do to override them more effectively, and how we can work *with* the brain to develop higher level inclusion skills and competencies.

This book offers a new way forward, and provides a fundamentally new framework for working across differences in positive and respectful ways. Based on practical, brain-based strategies and tools, this new approach focuses on developing high level inclusion skills that reduce defensiveness, build trust and create higher level outcomes. Building on the neuroscience of appreciation in particular, this brain-based approach supports developing new levels of competency in demonstrating compassion, understanding, and open-mindedness over judgments, negativity and fear - even when the brain isn't inclined to go there on its own. Using these brain-based strategies and tools, we can maximize the ways the brain works for us in building inclusion skills, and in the process, strengthen the circuitry for a more inclusive brain.

The diversity within organizations is growing at an unparalleled rate. In a report based on McKinsey research on global workforce trends, the authors concur that over the next five years the global marketplace will become increasingly cross-cultural, multi-ethnic, multi-generational and have more women in senior leadership positions. For organizations to continue being successful, the authors maintain they will need to be at their best in every capacity – more innovation, less time to market, excellent customer responsiveness and product quality. The report then makes clear that for organizations to take advantage of these opportunities, they must have a workforce that is highly skilled in building relationships and working effectively across differences. Towards the end of the report, one of the authors laments "We certainly all have the mental capacities to envision it, but do we have the brains that can actually carry it out?"[1] Indeed.

Building effective brain skills is at the forefront of creating positive relationships with others who are very different from ourselves – even when those differences may initially cause us discomfort. With brain skills, we can learn to work across differences in ways that are respectful, foster creativity, and ensure that people feel valued for their unique contributions, and are able to perform at their highest levels. In this new brain-based approach, we can begin the work of shaping a more inclusive brain, and pave the way towards more cooperation, understanding and peace in the workplaces of today and tomorrow.

CHAPTER ONE

Why Good Intentions Are Not Enough

"It's not just me and it's not just you, this is all around the world."
- Paul Simon, The Myth Of Fingerprints

The Archeology Museum in Istanbul holds what is believed to be the oldest peace treaty in history, dating back to 1258 BCE. This treaty is considered to be the first recorded document expressing cooperation, non-aggression, and mutual assistance between two warring groups. When visiting Istanbul last year, we were excited to see it.

Looking at it, we were truly amazed. There it was, a big clump of rock with words written on it in Akkadian, the diplomatic language of its day. Discovered in 1906 in Anatolia, it is proof that as far back as 23 centuries ago, people could work out their differences and write a new plan of peace and cooperation on a rock. It was inspiring to see people with tremendous anger and fear towards each other get past their differences, give up their grudges and move forward. We found this very compelling and hopeful. To our dismay, however, the plaque underneath told more of the story.

It turns out that the warring tribes decided to set aside their differences and write a peace treaty for only one reason: to combine their armies to become more powerful and conquer a shared enemy. The oldest peace treaty in the world wasn't about peace at all. It was about putting aside differences in order to destroy a different, more threatening group. Throughout history, this pattern of different groups aligning and cooperating with one another only when there is a shared threat is ubiquitous. Neuroscience findings now shed new light on these tendencies of the human brain.

Dr. Joshua Greene Director of Harvard's Moral Cognition Lab and author of Moral Tribes: Emotion, Reason and the Gap Between Us and Them, describes the evolution of cooperation in the brain, and shows how cooperation evolved *within* groups, but it did not evolve *between* groups. The brain's social wiring is what helped us learn to work cooperatively with others in order to survive. However, Dr. Greene points out, while our brains evolved circuitry that provided a strong ability to cooperate with others, this social wiring only evolved "within" groups and towards people who we perceived to be similar to ourselves; it did not evolve between groups we perceived as different from ourselves.

This basic wiring is alive and well in our brains today. For example, neuroscience findings show that when subjects view photographs of people who look like them, the areas in the brain for cooperation, empathy, and self-awareness are engaged. When subjects are shown photographs of people who don't look like them, these same brain areas are not activated as strongly or in some cases, not engaged at all.[2] This means that when we meet someone whose differences the brain perceives as familiar and comfortable, we are more inclined to move towards that person and create connections and build trust.

However, when we meet someone and the brain doesn't like their differences - the way they think, the color of their skin, what they believe, how they dress, where they worship, how they vote, their job level, the department they're from, or any other characteristics the brain perceives as outside its comfort zone - this is no small event. When the brain registers differences as discomfort, it sends an "away" impulse, and even regards these differences as potential threats.[3] Through the "us vs. them" base instincts in the brain, we unconsciously categorize people who look different from us as a threat (foe) or unconsciously favor someone who we perceive to be more like us (friend). These built-in brain tendencies unconsciously frame our world in ways that lead to creating 'in groups" and "out groups." Our brains are spring loaded to see the world through filters of "us vs. them" before we make a conscious decision about the people we meet.

From neuroscience we are learning that the brain actually predisposes us to see the world through a lens of inequity toward others. Every day in the workplace, the brain is automatically categorizing people based on their differences or their similarities, and whether these cause us comfort or discomfort. The brain's inherent biases set us up to unconsciously send verbal and non-verbal messages to some individuals that they are an "us" and we include them, while we send messages to others that they are a "them" and we exclude them. This goes on under the radar of our conscious awareness, and all of it directly impacts our behavior.

From an evolutionary standpoint, our brains are not positioned well for inclusion. The impulses that were once the hallmarks of our survivability are now getting in the way of our ability to respectfully engage with others who don't share our same life experiences, beliefs, attitudes, motivations and desires. This is what Greene calls "the tragedy of commonsense morality." We are learning that the brain's base instincts are fundamentally out of line with the needs of our current work places - and our world. By relying on a brain that gives us information about others that in the majority of cases is not helpful, our opportunity to successfully operate in the new world of increasing diversity is at risk. Dr. Greene acknowledges this, and goes on to say that in order to live peacefully with others whose beliefs and values may be threatening to our own, we have to learn to override what our base instincts may be telling us, and that this process can feel counter-intuitive to the brain.[4]

Neuroscience findings also reveal some very good news. Namely, that we can intentionally influence the brain's capacity to be more inclusive. We can learn and practice brain-based strategies and tools that strengthen the social brain's built-in circuitry for empathy and understanding, and practice these capacities with others who are not like us. We can learn brain skills that support the social brain's inherent capacities for compassion, care and collaboration, and extend these towards others in ways that support building respectful and inclusive relationships across differences, even when those differences cause us discomfort. To do this, it is helpful to have a better understanding of both new neuroscience findings underlying our biases and new findings about the circuitry of the social brain. Understanding these findings will help us more successfully challenge the brain's counter-intuitive stance towards inclusion and develop more positive relationships across differences.

Base Instincts: "Us vs. Them"

The "Us" Bias

Dr. Srini Pillay, a Harvard Medical and Business School Professor, suggests that working across differences is a "biological challenge," and that this biological challenge is rooted in the brain's preference for similarities. According to Dr. Pillay, "we are wired to recognize and process familiar people and situations from a young age," and he cites research demonstrating that young children recognize faces of their own race more quickly than those of different races. The brain's bias towards familiar faces also extends into adulthood. For adults, it takes only 200 milliseconds to unconsciously register whether a face is familiar or not, and recent research shows us that we process familiar faces with almost double the efficiency than unfamiliar faces. The brain clearly responds more quickly to those it recognizes as more familiar. It is wired to make this determination entirely on its own, with no conscious participation on our part.[5]

Dr. Jennifer Gutsell of the Social Interaction and Motivation Lab at Brandeis University has studied "motor resonance" in the brain. Motor resonance occurs when we watch another person's actions and it produces very similar brain activity in our brains - as if we'd performed the same action ourselves. Dr. Gutsell's research shows that subjects' brains only registered motor resonance when watching people who looked similar to themselves performing an action. This same motor resonance was not evident when subjects watched others outside of their ethnic group perform the same actions.6

People also showed resonant brain activity when observing emotions in others from the same cultural or ethnic group. When members of the same ethnic groups observed sadness in members of their own group, their brains also registered sadness. When observing sadness in people of different ethnic groups, however, there was no affective resonance observed. Researchers also found that the lack of resonance effects were even more pronounced when strong dislike and prejudice towards a group were also present.7 These studies demonstrate how the brain unconsciously processes the world through the lens of "us vs. them" and underscores the importance of learning to work with the brain to advance inclusion across differences, as the brain is not likely to go there on its own.

The "us" bias, and the unconscious preference for similarities, is also a strong, but often overlooked, contributor to discrimination in the workplace. In a literature review of studies on discrimination over five decades, the authors conclude that an "us" bias was a prominent, yet often unrecognized, factor in discrimination. In reviewing hundreds of scientific studies and surveys on discrimination, the authors state that there were "very many cases of discrimination not caused by an intention to harm people different from us, but by ordinary favoritism directed at helping people similar to ourselves." While the report also cited substantial evidence of intentional discrimination involving "inflicting harm and hostility," the authors maintain that "favoritism" is also a prevalent factor in discrimination and should be included as a component of discrimination research. Particularly, given the overwhelming evidence that favoritism is a strong unconscious brain tendency which also has the effect of inflicting harm, albeit unintentionally.

We see examples of the "us" bias in organizations every day. The "us" bias shows up in ways that can be deeply embedded into systems, preferred ways of working, and even what success looks like. For example, hiring practices are often filled with a preference for similarity, even within organizations that espouse a commitment to diversity. Research on hiring practices by the recruiting site *Indeed* found that 37% of managers who attended prestigious universities preferred to hire candidates with a similar educational background, whereas only 6% of managers and leaders who did not attend a prestigious university preferred to hire a candidate who did.[8] In recruitment, the similarity bias easily results in hiring practices that reinforce and promote sameness while shrinking the pool of available talented candidates, and reduces the organization's opportunities for new ideas and innovation. The CEO of Outmatch, a software recruiting company, stated in an interview with Business News Daily, "It's human nature; employers use their gut reactions to job candidates and hire people like themselves that they get along with."[9] Developing an awareness of the "us" bias is essential in overriding and minimizing its impact on individuals and organizations.

The "Them" Bias

Research shows that it only takes 50 milliseconds to register someone's gender when we first see them and only twice that long to note their racial background, before we immediately retreat to basic evolutionary principles.[10] In one study, for example, researchers scanned the brains of subjects as they reviewed pictures of what they perceived as "in group" and "out group" individuals. When viewing the "out group" pictures, the prefrontal cortex - the part of the brain necessary for cognition, self-management and engaging empathy - was less active than when viewing "in group" pictures. Moreover, when the subjects viewed individuals they perceived as "out, out groups" such as drug addicts and the homeless, there was no activity in the areas of cognition and self-management at all. Instead, these pictures activated the insula and amygdala, a pattern consistent with disgust. The authors go on to say that there is now "considerable neural evidence to support the prediction that extreme out-groups may be perceived as less than human, or dehumanized".[11]

Other studies also show the brain's "them" bias creates a tendency to associate differences that make us uncomfortable with attitudes of "less than." In one study involving brain scans paired with subjects' reported attitudes and beliefs, researchers found that "out-group" individuals were perceived as "being less able to experience complex human emotions, share in-group beliefs, or act according to societal norms, moral rules, and values." The authors state "that while individuals may consciously see members of social out-groups as people, the brain processes social out-groups as something less than human, whether we are aware of it or not."[12] In fact, they maintain that brain imaging provides a more accurate depiction of prejudice than the verbal reporting usually used in research studies.

We see the profoundly negative impact of the "them" bias every day. The news is filled with examples of intolerance towards differences, and shows us how the brain's defensive, threat-based tendencies can develop into full blown prejudice, hostility and hatred towards others simply based on their differences. The rise of terrorist groups, mass murder of gays, rising anti-Semitism, an increasing number of police shootings of unarmed black men and boys in the U.S., rising anti-Muslim sentiment, and an increasing number of sexual assaults on women on college campuses are in the news every day, and affecting our unconscious notions about people's differences. Whether it is someone's race, sexual orientation, gender identity, religious affiliation, or any dimension of difference, the impact of prejudices and acts of hatred are cruel, unbelievably disheartening, and need to be addressed at the societal level. These prejudices and hatreds also exist in the workplace, although they are most often hidden because stating them explicitly is grounds for termination in most organizations. But they are still there.

The "them" bias affects students as well. A study conducted at Duke in the spring of 2016 looked at incidents of discrimination on their campus. The Task Force on Bias and Hate Issues found that underrepresented student groups, such as people of color, LGBTQ+, certain religions, and women reported the highest rates of experiencing bias, hate and discrimination. Sixty percent of the women and 77% of the black students reported experiencing some form of discrimination or microaggressions "a few times per month" or more. The students also experienced a recurring lack of access to social and economic opportunities on campus. The report goes on to state that the incidents profoundly impacted the students by causing strong feelings of exclusion. Feeling excluded diminished the diverse students' sense of being valued and created concerns for their safety on campus. It also resulted in a number of serious mental health problems, and generated skepticism about whether Duke had been sufficiently serious in addressing these matters.[13]

Another recent example of the "them" bias involves a lawsuit against the Hudson City Savings bank for "redlining" African American and Hispanic neighborhoods in New York, New Jersey, and Connecticut. (Redlining is a word based on the way banks and insurance companies used to draw red map lines around the neighborhoods of color they didn't want to sell to.) Even though the practice has been illegal for decades, Hudson City Savings continued the practice. In 2014, the bank approved a total of 1,886 mortgages, but only 25 of those mortgages were for African Americans. Settling out of court for $33 million, the Consumer Financial Protection Bureau and the Justice Department said it was the largest settlement for redlining in both departments' history.[14]

Understanding that the brain is inherently wired towards sameness and against differences means that we need to continually challenge systems, institutions, practices and policies that perpetuate favoritism and negative stereotypes and prejudices. It is absolutely imperative to continue working hard to eradicate unlawful and immoral practices aimed at people's differences. To do this effectively it is also essential that we learn to manage our own brains.

Dr. Arne Roets, a lead researcher in the psychology of prejudice, suggests that looking at prejudice through the brain makes us think differently about how and why people become prejudiced, and what to do about it. She maintains that to reduce prejudice, we need to first acknowledge that it is in all of us because it arises from the brain's need to quickly categorize and make sense of the world. She goes on to say social categories are useful to the brain for reducing complexity, but the problem arises when we then "assign conditioned narratives to these categories which then leads to stereotyping and prejudices."[15] These conditioned narratives are often unconscious and automatic, yet, as we've seen, they our impact attitudes and behaviors toward others.

The Brain and Bias

Neuroscience is now making it clear that having biases and forming stereotypes that result in prejudiced and exclusionary behaviors is an inevitable result of the way the brain works. This is a phenomenal discovery. It is now a basic fact of science that the brain doesn't provide a level playing field when it comes to our unconscious perceptions and reactions to others. Whether it's someone's ethnicity, their political beliefs, how they dress, where they worship, whether they have an accent, their sexual orientation, or their level in the organization, the brain unconsciously filters differences through a lens of whether they are more like us or less like us, and this then registers as comfortable or uncomfortable in the brain. According to Rutgers University researchers Laurie Rudman and Richard Ashmore, our brains develop shortcuts for social identification so that we can swiftly categorize others and avoid the energy-intensive processing of conscious thought. Often we do not even realize how extensively subconscious stereotypes (positive and negative) shape our reactions."[16]

The brain is inherently predisposed to *not view* others with equal regard. Moreover, these unconscious filters in the brain are not the purview of any one group. Everyone's brain unconsciously filters the world through an "us vs. them" lens including the stories and stereotypes that go with them. Whether you are Caucasian, African-American, American Indian,

Latino, or a part of any other social, cultural, racial or ethnic group, your brain has unconscious biases for and against others. The scientific fact is that our brains are all wired as bias making machines. Understanding this is actually good news as it helps us move away from the "good person/ bad person" paradigm of diversity, which allows us to have more honest and authentic dialogue across differences.

We have known for a long time that we all exhibit biases towards others. What science is now making clear is that while our biases are related to our past conditioning, they actually go much deeper than that. The brain shows us the world through filters that are built into its operating system, and this means we can never uncover all of our biases. Science is showing us that we can have both a conscious brain that believes in diversity and inclusion, and an unconscious brain that is biased - for or against - people's differences. People will sometimes say, "No, I'm not like that. I am very open minded and I accept all people." This might be someone's intention, and they may be better than average at overcoming these brain tendencies, but the brain has millennia of practice creating in and out groups, and under the radar of our conscious awareness these brain dynamics still influence our behavior today. Physicist Leonard Mlodinow, observes in his book, "Subliminal: How Your Unconscious Mind Rules Your Behavior," that while the brain has developed over millions of years, we have actually only lived in civilized society for less than 1 percent of that time. He goes on to say that we're walking around with a brain inside our skulls that operates from the Stone Age, but is now full of twenty-first-century knowledge.[17]

Towards a More Inclusive Brain

It is becoming clear that to successfully advance diversity and inclusion in the workplace, the brain needs our help. To recognize and override the brain's built-in biases, we need to *intentionally* work with the brain, because without our conscious involvement, the brain won't go there on its own. Left to its own devices, the brain's preference for comfort over discomfort will prevail, and our opportunity for evolving a more inclusive brain will be lost. To succeed in our increasingly diverse workplaces, individuals need to know how to override the brain's discomfort with differences, go out of pattern, and move towards discovering what connects them with others. With this knowledge, it is now possible to intentionally shape a more inclusive brain.

Shaping a more inclusive brain is about challenging our biases and assumptions, and it is also about being willing to regard someone openly in order to learn about who they are, and what is important and meaningful for them. Focusing on what connects us engages our curiosity and a willingness to learn something new and authentic about a person, and provides an alternative narrative to any stereotypical storylines, negative assumptions or judgments we may have. While this can feel extremely counter-intuitive to the brain, there is also no way around it. We can either learn to go beyond the brain's discomfort and build connections, understanding, and trust across differences, or we can resort to our base instincts and continue getting more of what we already have: unmanaged "us vs. them" dynamics. Based on what science is telling us, consciously cooperating across differences is what sets the neurological conditions for a new, more inclusive future; one that is based on identifying shared interests and valuing outcomes that draw the circle of "we" ever larger.

There is actually circuitry available that we can develop and strengthen across differences to build a more inclusive brain. The brain already has the essential circuitry and wiring to cooperate and build social bonds with others, and this social circuitry developed most strongly towards people the brain perceived to be more like us. Yet, we now have the knowledge and opportunity to strengthen and extend these capacities towards others who are outside our comfort zone, and whom the brain may initially regard as a "them." We can consciously pay attention to building connections and trust with others who don't share our same culture, language, age, gender, race, values or life experiences. By learning brain-based tools, strategies and skills, we can strengthen the brain's built-in social capacities and extend these across differences.

Strengthening the social capacities of the brain matters for another important reason as well. From neuroscience we are learning that every person's brain - regardless of their differences - has a survival-based need for inclusion. Matthew Lieberman, author of "Social: Why Our Brains Are Wired to Connect" and Director of the UCLA Social Cognitive Neuroscience lab, shows how our brains have a strong survival-based need to belong, and how the brain developed the ability to join and cooperate with others to increase our collective ability to survive. According to Dr. Lieberman, the brain's deeply embedded social circuitry is what made it possible for us to become smarter by working together, and it has also created a basic human need for group belonging. The social wiring in the brain is what establishes our primary need for inclusion. Dr. Lieberman goes on to say that "the human need to belong and connect with others is even more fundamental than our need for food or shelter."[18] A feeling of belonging and being a valued member of the group is not just nice to have; it is a brain requirement for survival and to feel and operate at our best. When this need is not met, the brain isn't able to function or perform at its optimum levels. Research studies show, for example, that being excluded actually interferes with the process of creating and connecting neurons in the brain in a process called myelination, which is essential in learning new skills and behaviors.[19]

It is through the social brain that we receive information about people's intentions, attitudes and feelings which provides us with an empathetic window into our shared concerns and needs. Research also shows that we can intentionally increase the brain's capacity for empathy. In a study by neuroscientists at the D'Or Institute for Research and Education in Brazil, for example, volunteers were instructed to engage in feelings of empathy while inside a functional magnetic resonance machine. As they did so, the researchers monitored their brain patterns. Afterwards, the subjects received feedback about their brain activity which helped them pinpoint when their feelings of empathy were highest. They were then scanned a second time, and by applying this learning a majority were able to intentionally increase their empathic brain patterns.[20]

Increasing our ability to extend empathy doesn't mean we have to agree with someone, or that we even share similar experiences. Showing empathy is more than simply identifying and repeating people's feelings. It can include that, but it also involves listening with your whole self in a way that communicates sincerity, builds trust, and encourages deeper conversations. Showing empathy involves recognizing that people's perceptions *are* their reality, even if we don't see it the same way. By developing and strengthening the social brain across differences we can increase our capacity to listen outside of what we already know, and build connections and understanding with others who don't share our same culture, language, age, gender, race, values or life experiences. By consciously working with the social brain, we can increase our ability to extend the "us" circle ever wider, and create work environments where everyone feels included and safe to be who they are without fear of judgments or recriminations, and are motivated to contribute at their highest level. We can build the circuitry of the social brain through conscious intentions and actions.

Neuroplasticity and Inclusion

Brain science is showing us that what we focus on and where we put our energy and attention actually shapes the brain itself. Called neuroplasticity, it is now well established that the brain is malleable and changes physically in response to our thoughts, feelings, and actions. Through studies on the brain's "plasticity" and ability to change, it's becoming increasingly clear that we can build a more inclusive brain through the choices we make. When we consciously and consistently choose to act in new more inclusive ways, we are both overriding the brain's "us vs. them" tendencies, as well as setting the stage for establishing more inclusive habits and patterns in our behavior.

For centuries it was believed that the brain was fixed by early adulthood. It is now well established that our brains continue to change and build new connections throughout our lives. In fact, re-wiring the brain is how we grow and change, and bring about new mental, emotional and behavioral habits. Dr. Norman Doidge describes neuroplasticity as "the most important breakthrough in our understanding of the brain in four hundred years."[21] Neuroplasticity is what makes it possible for us to consciously influence the physical wiring as well as the unconscious habits of our brains.

Being able to consciously influence the physical wiring of the brain provides a new juncture in our evolution. We are now in the unparalleled position of being able to actively participate in creating a brain that is more inclusive. Referred to as "self-directed neuroplasticity," the following example in particular shows the powerful opportunities that can result from the brain's ability to rewire itself.

The Institutes for the Achievement of Human Potential is an organization that specializes in working with children with a broad range of brain injuries and disabilities to capitalize on brain plasticity and help the brain forge new neuropathways. They have discovered that *repetition, frequency* and *duration* are the three critical success factors to re-wiring the brain. Using their brain-based therapies, children with brain injuries that were blind regain sight, children who could not hear begin to hear, and children who have been in comas are able to walk and run and regain their abilities.[22] Neuroplasticity pertains equally to adults.

Dr. Richard Davidson, Director of the Waisman Laboratory for Brain Imaging and Behavior at the University of Wisconsin, explains that the brain's plasticity and ability to change is actually the rule rather than the exception. He states that "what we focus on is what we get," and maintains that the critical success component in today's world comes down to being able to choose which influences are we going to pay attention to.[23] To effectively engage in self-directed neuroplasticity, however, requires that we understand a particular part of the brain called the prefrontal cortex.

The Prefrontal Cortex and New Skills Going Forward

The prefrontal cortex — what we are calling the higher brain - is a part of the neocortex, and is the newest part of the brain to have developed. The higher brain is what give us conscious awareness and the ability to "think about our thinking", and it is where the competency of inclusion lies. From a diversity and inclusion perspective, it is the higher brain that gives us both the capacity to recognize and override biases, and also the ability to consciously direct our attention towards open-mindedness, empathy, and collaboration over the brain's inherent biases. David Amodio, in an article titled "The Egalitarian Brain," explains that while it may be impossible to eradicate our biases, the brain is thoroughly equipped and capable of overriding them. He explains that we can work with the brain to build and strengthen our capacity for connecting, collaborating and building trust across differences. Dr. Amodio identifies the role of the higher brain in this process, and states that to become more egalitarian and successfully override biases and prejudices in the brain, "we need to train ourselves to help the neocortex to do its job."[24]

Prefrontal Cortex

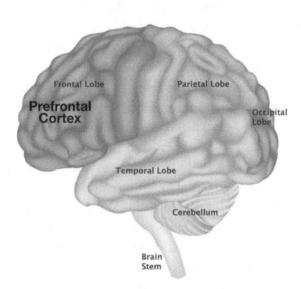

The higher brain plays a critical role in our ability to demonstrate the following key competencies of inclusion:

- Consider others' perspectives, needs and feelings
- Choose empathy and understanding over judgments, biases and stereotypes

- Understand the impact of our behavior on others
- Create connections with others outside of our comfort zone
- Consciously override old behavior patterns and establish new behavior habits
- Stay focused and open-minded even under pressure and stress
- Choose positivity and appreciation-based strategies for advancing more collaborative working environments
- Engage curiosity and a willingness to learn
- Listen outside of what we already know
- Positively influence the brain for higher engagement levels
- Understand we can be well intended, but our behavior can still be biased

While the prefrontal cortex is critical to developing inclusion skills and competencies, it also presents a central challenge that can't be ignored. The prefrontal cortex is easily destabilized and goes offline without our awareness that it has even happened. The brain has deeply embedded, survival-based needs for comfort, certainty and predictability. Intentionally engaging across differences in new ways can pose a direct threat to the brain's baseline instincts, and these threats (real or perceived) can easily destabilize the higher brain and take it offline. When the higher brain goes offline, we lose self-awareness and the ability to make conscious choices. We lose access to the competencies that make it possible for us to notice and challenge our assumptions and biases, effectively undermining any good intentions. We lose the ability to see and understand multiple perspectives, and our motivation to consciously create connections with individuals who are outside of our comfort zone is significantly diminished. When the prefrontal cortex goes offline, not only do we lose our capacity to be inclusive, we also lose the ability to consciously engage in directing and shaping a more inclusive brain.

So it is a bit of a catch twenty-two. We need the higher brain to make new choices and move towards what is unfamiliar and uncomfortable, and yet these are the very activities that can destabilize the higher brain and take it offline. As Dr. Amodio mentioned, we need to actively participate to help the neocortex do its job. In order to do this effectively, we need to understand the unconscious brain, and how we can work with it to stabilize the prefrontal cortex, and make more conscious and inclusive choices more consistently. By understanding more about the unconscious brain and the defensive brain, we can learn tools and strategies to leverage these brain dynamics in overriding unconscious biases, and be able to more effectively and consistently engage in behaviors of respect and inclusion across differences. First, we will look understanding the unconscious brain and how we can target various unconscious processes in ways that result in positive inclusion norms and expectations in the work environment.

CHAPTER TWO

The Unconscious Brain and the Power of Appreciation

"Until you make the unconscious conscious,
it will direct your life and you will call it fate."
          - Carl Jung

During the 1980s there was a famous study done with nursing home patients who spent two weeks living in a fabricated home environment. Referred to as the "counter clockwise" study, it was designed to look at the psychological and physiological effects that occur in elderly people when they return to an environment that reminds them of an earlier time in their lives. For two weeks participants lived in a home that was an exact replica of a house from the 1950s, a time in their lives when they would have been in their mid-thirties. Everything from the wallpaper, appliances, furniture, newspapers, music, soaps and clothing were original or a perfect replica from that era. The only instruction the patients received was to think and speak only in the present tense, and to share lots of memories from this time in their lives. The participants were not given any other information about their situation to avoid a "placebo effect."

At the end of two weeks, the physiological and psychological measurements that had been taken at the beginning of the study showed significant improvements. Overall participants showed greater improvement in joint flexibility, finger length (a result of diminished arthritis) and manual dexterity than the control group. The 1950s immersion group also showed improvements in both memory and hearing as well as improvements in posture and height that did not occur in the control group. On the psychological side, 63 percent increased their scores on intelligence tests, and most showed remarkable improvements in mental energy, outlook and confidence compared with the control group. Measures such as blood pressure, heart rate and immune system markers all showed significant improvements as well, leading some researchers to call the participants "younger" at the end of the study.[25] This is one of many compelling studies that demonstrate the extent to which our unconscious brains pick up and record things in the environment that are outside of our awareness, and that impact us on every level: physical, mental and emotional.

This same unconscious process goes on in the workplace every day. Throughout the day the unconscious brain is picking up and registering what people do, how they do it, what they say, how they say it, how it feels, what behaviors get rewarded, what behaviors get punished, how to think, what to believe, who to trust, even how to stand, and what gestures to use to appear most credible. All of this directly influences our behavior. Neuroscientists estimate that the unconscious brain can pay attention to over 11 million bits of incoming sensory data every second from our surrounding environment (with some estimates even much higher), while the conscious brain can only pay attention to 40-50 environmental cues at a time.[26] Just like in the nursing home study, cues in the environment that we aren't consciously aware of directly impact our thoughts, feelings and behavior in the workplace.

In terms of inclusion, neuroscience is now revealing a new level of understanding about biases and the unconscious brain. It turns out that our biases towards differences exist within a larger set of unconscious processes in the brain. All of our attitudes and behaviors – not just those related to biases towards differences – get embedded so deeply in the circuitry of the brain that they are not only unconscious, but they get normalized by these and other brain processes. Our biases towards people's differences become camouflaged by the larger unconscious landscape and we don't think to examine or challenge them because they just feel normal and right, even if they don't make sense at a conscious, logical level.

Consider these statistics:

- Approximately 14.5 percent of men in the U.S. are over six feet tall. Among CEOs of Fortune 500 companies, that number is 58 percent.[27]
- In 2014, female full-time workers made only 79 cents for every dollar earned by men, a gender wage gap of 21 percent. The gap has narrowed only a few percent since it was first recorded in the 1970s.[28]
- Job applicants with white sounding names were 50 percent more likely to get called back for an interview than applicants with black sounding names. Later in the same study, researchers added additional credentials to some of the resumes. When they added more credentials to white candidates it increased their call back rate by 30 percent. When black candidates' resumes were given more credentials, it improved their call back rate by only 9 percent.[29]
- Black men are six times as likely to be incarcerated in federal and state prisons and local jails than white men, according to the U.S. Bureau of Justice Statistics report released in 2012.[30]
- Investors were 2-3 times more likely to invest in a new business idea if the man making the pitch was attractive.[31]

This is only a small list of the numerous unconscious biases that negatively impact people every day. Unconscious biases operate under the radar of conscious awareness, yet the impact can be just as negative and harmful as conscious or intentional biases. The unconscious brain is constantly registering all the messages that cause some individuals to feel included and valued, that they are an "us," and cause others to feel undervalued and excluded, that they are a "them." What can make unconscious bias particularly difficult is that it often results in some individuals experiencing severe discrimination, while others may not even notice that it is happening. Our personal experiences become so deeply embedded into the circuitry of our brains – and create such strong, unconsciously preferred states – that it can blind us to each other's very different experiences and realities. This is the nature of the unconscious brain. Our very different versions of normal get seared deeply into the brain and cause inclusion blindness.

Our unconscious habits and the brain's fallback position towards familiarity, ease and "normal" can be so compelling that we don't actually see outlying facts and situations – even when they are right in front of us. Research shows it is very possible to engage in discriminatory behavior without having any intent to discriminate or any conscious dislike for those who end up being disadvantaged by our behavior.[32] As we've seen, favoritism is an often overlooked factor in discrimination. The "us" bias is wired so deeply into the survival circuitry of our brains that – consciously and unconsciously – it draws us towards individuals and situations that are familiar, easy, feel "normal" and comfortable.

We have known for a long time that we all exhibit biases towards others. What science is now making clear is that while our biases are related to our past conditioning, it goes much deeper than that and our conditioning actually shapes the brain itself. Dr. David Eagleman, neuroscientist and author of the book, "Incognito: The Secret Lives of the Brain," talks about how all of the experiences and messages we are continually exposed to – such as our cultural conditioning – leave their signature in the circuitry of each individual brain. He uses an analogy of a single acorn to elucidate how everything in the environment leaves its mark on the brain.

Dr. Eagleman explains that by studying a single acorn in detail, we can learn a great deal about its surroundings – from its moisture content to the microbes involved, to the sunlight conditions of the larger forest. And like the acorn, each individual brain also reflects its surroundings in its structure. Our beliefs, ideas, opinions, customs, and what we consider to be normal ways of acting are all absorbed into the neural circuitry of our brains from the "social forest" around us. Neuroscience studies show, for example, that moral attitudes can be read from the physiological responses in the brains of people from different cultures.[33] Many other studies in the growing field of cultural neuroscience also demonstrate how deeply our cultural conditioning shapes the neural circuitry in the brain.

For example, one study involving U.S. Americans and Chinese participants showed how different cultural norms trigger different patterns of activity in the brain. In this study, both the U.S. American and Chinese participants were asked to think about the personal trait of honesty and whether they personally considered themselves to be honest, and then to consider whether another person, such as a close relative, is honest. The study found that the brain patterns between the U.S. American and Chinese participants were not the same. When the American participants thought about whether they personally are honest, their brain activity looked very different from when they were asked to think about if someone else is honest, even a close relative. In contrast, when the Chinese participants thought about whether they personally are honest, their brain activity looked almost identical to when they thought about whether someone else, such as a close relative, is honest.

For the U.S. participants there was a clear differentiation between self and others in the brain activity patterns that was not observed with the Chinese, who had no differentiation in their brain activity patterns between self and a close relative. Interestingly, this finding correlates to behavioral studies on cultural differences that show that U.S. Americans have a strong cultural trait of individualism and focus on individual strengths and attributes, whereas the Chinese tend to have a strong cultural trait for collectivism and being deeply connected to others. This and other studies illustrate that people can see or think about the exact stimulus and have completely different neural responses. University of Texas psychologist Denise Park, who has conducted several cultural neuroscience studies, states that her greatest hope is that these studies will build awareness that people may not be talking about the same thing, even if they are looking at the same thing.[34]

Our conditioning shapes what our brain sees and how we interpret it, and is embedded into the neural-circuitry of our world view causing us to equate what is familiar and comfortable with the "right" way to think and act. The brain structurally arranges our world as "normal," which sets us up to misinterpret each other's intentions and actions, and easily impedes our awareness of what is actually happening for others. Our sense of normal can also impede our motivation to learn about differences and manage our own behaviors.

We now know that the brain operates on unconscious processes all by itself without any involvement from our conscious self and that the brain shows us the world through filters that are built into its operating system. These unconscious dynamics result in deeply embedded assumptions and biases, and this also means that we can never uncover all of our biases. The brain essentially is a bias making machine, and this information provides a new start point for individuals to be honest and willing to look at and discuss their biases. The more willing each person is to own they are biased, the more they will also be able to notice, manage, and override biases effectively.

In this new brain-based approach to inclusion, we gain a deeper understanding of how unconscious processes work, and how we can *work with* the unconscious brain. Operating with more understanding of how unconscious processes work, we can now positively influence the work environment and the unconscious brain in ways that help us be more inclusive. This new approach combines findings on the unconscious brain with the neuroscience of appreciation. It involves incorporating appreciation-based strategies and tools into one's daily work routine and sending positive and consistent inclusion messages into the environment that prime the unconscious brain positively and create new operating norms. This appreciation-based approach also strongly supports strengthening the social brain, and building new neuropathways that ensure long-term, positive inclusion behaviors and habits. Before getting into how to consciously influence the unconscious brain in ways that foster inclusion, it is helpful to understand more about the unconscious brain and how it operates.

Understanding the Unconscious Brain

Recognizing and managing unconscious biases is obviously a tricky process because we can't manage what we don't see. As such, it is helpful to understand some key processes underlying the unconscious brain to be able to increase our awareness and manage our biases more effectively. Additionally, we can then target these unconscious processes and intentionally leverage them for more inclusion. There are four aspects of the unconscious brain in particular that when better understood provide us with new strategies to manage unconscious bias and foster inclusion. These are: Priming, the Reticular Activating System (RAS), Neuropathways, and Heuristics.

It is also important to note that it is not our intent to present a complete neuroscience of the unconscious brain. In fact, neuroscientists state explicitly that they themselves have only reached the tip of the iceberg in their full understanding of the unconscious brain. Instead, our overview of the unconscious brain focuses on the aspects that directly influence inclusion abilities and skills, and that can also be re-worked to influence the unconscious brain positively to advance inclusion norms and behaviors in the workplace.

Priming

Priming involves implicit memory and shows how the unconscious brain picks up and pays attention to things in the environment that effect or "prime" our behavior in certain ways. Priming is responsible for the odd experience of learning a new word and then suddenly seeing it again, or buying a new car and suddenly noticing ten cars on the road exactly like yours, or learning you're pregnant and the world suddenly fills up with pregnant ladies. The unconscious brain has always been aware of these things in the environment. The new word that keeps showing up, the hundreds of cars you see on the road that are the same as yours, and the pregnant women were always there, but they are only let into our conscious awareness once we already know about them. Our brain has been primed to now notice these specific things.

We saw in the nursing home study how priming the subjects' unconscious brains influenced them on every level: physical, mental and emotional. Another aspect of priming the unconscious brain is that it works amazingly fast. A clear example of this can be seen in a study involving shoppers in a supermarket choosing a bottle of wine. In this study, shoppers passed by a display containing four French wines and four German wines that were all comparable in price and characteristics. On alternating days, either French or German music was played at the wine display. On the days the German music played, 73 percent of the wine bought was German. On the days the French music played, 77 percent of the wine purchased was French. After making their decisions and purchasing their wine, shoppers were stopped and asked if the music had influenced their decision; 86 percent of the shoppers said, "Music? What music?"[35] This is one of hundreds of studies that demonstrate how fast the unconscious brain picks up cues in the environment we are unaware of, but then have an immediate impact on our behavior, decisions and expectations.

A classic study by Yale psychologist John Bargh demonstrates not only how quickly the unconscious brain is primed, it also shows how priming directly and unconsciously influences our behavior. In this study, students were given a list of words to read before going to a colleague to ask for their next assignment. One group was given positive, respectful words like "appreciate," "patiently," and "respect," while the other group was given disrespectful words like "rude," "aggressively," "disturb," and "intrude." The study included an unexpected delay that the students weren't told about. When they went to get their next assignment, they were told they would have to wait ten minutes until the colleague they needed to talk to was off the phone. The researchers then observed the students' behavior as they waited. The results showed that the waiting behaviors between the two groups was indeed very different.

The group that got the positive words exhibited positively associated behaviors. They waited patiently with positive expressions and attitudes, and almost no one from this group interrupted the conversation. The second group that got the list of disrespectful behaviors and was primed to be rude was markedly different in their behaviors. They were much quicker to become irritated and interrupt the conversation, on average after just about five minutes. Reading a list of words created unconscious associated behaviors. In this study, the students' unconscious brains were "primed" to behave in certain ways by exposure to words unconsciously associated with different kinds of behaviors.[36]

In the workplace, we are constantly being primed by the verbal and non-verbal behaviors of those around us. The priming process happens very quickly based on only the smallest of cues, and these can feed directly into unconscious biases. For example, neuroscience studies show that new biases can be formed in the brain in as little as 2 or 3 exposures to an image, message, or associated ideas.[37] Our brains are being primed to think, feel and act in ways that directly impact the verbal and nonverbal messages we unconsciously send. In the workplace, priming has a powerful impact because it often includes the unconscious micro-messages we send that cause people to feel included and valued or excluded and minimized.

Priming Behaviors: Inclusion and Exclusion

Microinequities and microaffirmations are terms used to describe the small verbal and nonverbal behaviors, gestures and messages in the workplace that contribute to someone feeling excluded (microinequities) or to someone feeling included (microaffirmations). Both kinds are very often unconscious behaviors that mirror the norms of the work environment. On the microaffirmation side, it is inclusionary behaviors and gestures such as smiling and keeping eye contact while someone is talking, asking for someone's opinion, showing support, sharing information and acknowledging someone's input. Microinequities, on the other hand, involve exclusionary behaviors, words, and small gestures such as rolling your eyes, ignoring someone's idea in a meeting, consistently forgetting someone's name, or not paying full attention to someone when they speak. These small verbal and nonverbal behaviors are all examples of the micro-messages we unconsciously send about who is a "more than" and who is a "less than." Whether it is microinequities or microaffirmations, these gestures and behaviors in the work environment unconsciously prime people to treat some individuals with respect, while others get marginalized and treated with a demonstrated lack of respect.

A recent study of physicians underscores the impact of nonverbal messages and priming. The study examined physician-patient interaction in time-pressured, end of life situations and found that the physicians gave less compassionate nonverbal cues when treating black patients compared to white patients. What is of particular interest is that the physicians' spoken words were the same to both the black and white patients; what was markedly different was their nonverbal communication. When the physicians were communicating with the white patients, they generally stood right next to the bed and touched the patient in a sympathetic manner, sending a nonverbal message of compassion and care. These same nonverbal communications were not observed with black patients. The physicians generally stood farther away, held a clipboard, and did not touch the patient. This disparity in nonverbal communication feeds directly into the unconscious brain, and can easily trigger feelings of being marginalized. The study's senior author, Amber Barnato MD, MPH, highlights this, stating that "Poor nonverbal communication – something the physician may not even be aware he or she is doing – could explain why many black patients perceive discrimination in the health care setting."[38]

In a Profiles in Diversity Journal article, "The DNA of Culture Change," Joyce Tucker states it this way: "In any given conversation, we send hundreds of messages, often without even saying a word. Just as television or radio waves surround us yet we never see them, these micro-messages are just as pervasive and nearly as difficult to discern."[39] The words we use or don't use, and all the unconscious nonverbal messages we send, unknowingly impact people at a deep level. When these messages come from leaders or others in positions of influence, they are particularly impactful because a leader's behavior also primes others to treat someone in the same way the leader treats them - positively or negatively. In one client situation, we saw this happen on a team.

A new person was hired who brought specific technical skills that expanded the team's capacities. Many experienced members of the team did not believe that the new person's training and experience was as important or as valuable as their own. Without being conscious of this bias, the more senior team members engaged in microinequities towards the new person, behaviors such as not considering his ideas or including him in formal project meetings, and displaying non-verbal gestures of intolerance in front of him and others on the team. Eventually the other team members started mirroring the more senior team members' behaviors, and the new person's "lack of qualifications" became a repeated story about him. The more he tried to be proactive and change their beliefs about him, the more it contributed to people's negative impressions. The story took on a life of its own, creating a downward spiral for the new person, and the opportunity for him to contribute his talents and abilities was lost to the team.

When an organization's culture is weighted more towards these small, often unconscious behaviors of exclusion, or microinequities, this not only impacts engagement and performance, but also peoples' physical and mental health. For example, research conducted by the University of Texas suggests that both subtle and overt biases impact women's leadership engagement to such an extent it can lead to depression. Tetyana Pudrovska, lead author of the study, states that "Women leaders are viewed as being less competent than men, they're evaluated in performance reviews on personality traits while men are evaluated on accomplishments, and they're interrupted more often during team meetings." She goes on to say that the day-to-day interactions can become so tiring to deal with that it's like "death by 10,000 paper cuts."[40]

As social beings, we have a primary survival-based need to belong, feel accepted and included. When this experience is withheld or when we are given mixed messages about our value, it is disruptive to our systems: mental, emotional and physical. The pain of social exclusion in the workplace engenders fear, creates disengagement, and undermines performance. For historically marginalized groups, such as people of color, women, LGBTQ+, or those with disabilities, these negative effects can be cumulative and this can cause strong reactions to even very small messages of exclusion. People who don't have a history of being marginalized sometimes view these strong reactions as an overreaction to what appears to be a minor or insignificant gesture or use of language. And yet, neuroscience findings show that social pain registers in the brain in the same place as physical pain. When people have been consistently treated in ways that cause social exclusion, a strong emotional reaction is understandable. We need to appreciate that social pain is real pain; it is not people being "overly sensitive." When there are strong emotional reactions to behaviors of exclusion, we need to respond with compassion, seek to understand, and work on becoming more aware of the micro-messages we send, and their impact others, so we can be more successful in changing our behavior.

When ongoing micro-messages of exclusion become normalized ways of behaving, they get embedded into "the way we do things around here." Individuals who are treated as "less thans" and excluded by these patterns are often *very conscious* of them. Excluded individuals can also find it difficult and incredibly frustrating to try and get others who are not impacted by these patterns to become aware of them. From neuroscience, we now know that the unconscious brain filters information to the conscious brain based on what we know. If a person has never experienced significant marginalization and/or thought about it a lot, it can be difficult for them to really "hear" and understand someone's description of what caused them to feel excluded. Therefore, it becomes imperative to seek to understand the experiences of others, spend additional effort and energy learning and becoming more aware of patterns of exclusion and their impact on others, and to be open to feedback about the negative impact of our own behaviors.

Reticular Activating System

We like to think that we are in control of what we consciously pay attention to. However, research on the unconscious brain reveals this is not the case, and the unconscious brain exerts much more influence on what we notice and don't notice than we realize. This happens in part through the brain's Reticular Activating System (RAS), which, in addition to regulating aspects of motor control and sleep wake states, is involved in filtering information from the unconscious brain into our conscious awareness. The filtering process of the RAS is sometimes compared to the role of a bouncer at a night club that works on behalf of the brain. It selects what information is let into the conscious mind and what information gets filtered out. According to neuroscience, the information we perceive in our awareness is not created, nor is it reacted to, by conscious processes. Instead, conscious awareness can be referred to as a "middle-man" that doesn't do as much work as we think.[41]

All day, our sensory organs are bombarded with massive amounts of information, and the RAS acts as a gatekeeper of our attentional resources. Researchers at the University of Pennsylvania, for instance, have discovered that the human eye transmits about 10 million bits per second to the brain,[42] and eyesight accounts for just one of our senses. With all the incoming sensory data, the RAS distinguishes between relevant information and irrelevant information – directly relaying to the conscious mind what to pay attention to. It plays a critical role in how the brain learns to ignore repetitive, meaningless stimuli yet be responsive to other stimuli. It also plays an important role in the process of priming.

This accounts for experiences such as a person being able to sleep right through the din of loud traffic every night, but wake up suddenly if they hear their young child make a sound in the middle of the night. Or the experience of being in a loud crowded room engaged in a conversation, when all of a sudden you hear your name mentioned across the room. Essentially, we learn to stop responding to stimulus that is not pertinent and be responsive to what the brain deems to be highly important to each of us individually.

Our conditioning, experiences and beliefs all help the RAS determine what is important and relevant and what we can ignore. Our conditioned lenses of what is "normal" influence what information in our environment the brain determines we need to pay attention to or to disregard. For example, this is demonstrated in a study that looked at cultural differences in processing images. Conducted at the University of Texas, this study looked at the effects of culture on brain processing of Chinese and U.S. American participants. The researchers had the participants, while in a functional magnetic resonance imaging (fMRI), look at pictures of visual scenes. Some of the scenes were congruent, such as a cow in a field, and some of the scenes were incongruent, such as a picture of a cow in a kitchen. The study found that the Chinese participants showed more neural processing when the scenes were incongruent compared to the U.S. American participants.[43] The authors of the study noted these findings, consistent with other studies, showed that the Chinese culture tends to be a high context culture, paying attention to the entire scene, as the entire context is important. In contrast, the U.S. American culture tends to be more low context, and the U.S. American participants payed more attention to the individual object rather than the entire scene, even when it was incongruent. Cultural conditioning is one of many influences on what the brain deems important and listens to or not. This helps explain why in meetings for example, it's difficult for people to acknowledge and understand what is important to others when it does not even show up as relevant in their own brain.

Our experience of "normal" is such a strong and unconsciously preferred state that not only does it influence what the brain pays attention to, it also sets us up to see what we want to see, and as a result, completely miss the obvious. A colleague shared a story that highlights how this can happen. He was traveling in Ohio for business and went to see a public art installation he had heard about. The installation was a large sculpture that consisted of ears of corn sculptures in multiple rows, all made of cement. The following day he told his client that he got to see the sculpture and how impressive it was seeing all those rows of huge yellow ears of corn. The client looked at him quizzically for a moment, and replied "they are not yellow, they are cement that has not been painted." Our colleague was so certain they were yellow, he drove back for a second look that night and was thunderstruck to see that the ears of corn were indeed not yellow, but the color of unpainted cement. In his experience, yellow is the "normal" color of ears of corn, and that is what he saw, even though they were not. Our brains are so conditioned by our experiences of what is typical and "normal" that it can be very difficult to shift to a new way of thinking about the world around us. The strong pull of normal in the brain not only creates conditioned filters, it is also tied to our survival needs which involves being able to move fast and conserve energy at the same time.

Speed and Efficiency: The Unconscious Pull of Normal

Conserving energy is a main goal of the brain. The brain makes up only 2% of the body's total weight and yet it consumes 20-25% of the body's available energy every day.[44] Some neuroscientists even refer to the brain as an "energy hog." To conserve energy, the brain needs to be highly efficient, and one way it does this is by creating neuropathways. Neuropathways are formed in the brain by neurons in the brain physically connecting with each other. When we engage in a new thought or behavior, a chemical signal travels from one neuron (brain cell) to another neuron creating a physical connection between them. Then, the more we engage in the same thoughts, beliefs attitudes and behaviors, the stronger this connection becomes. Overtime, these strong neurological connections become well established neuropathways, and operate as high speed expressways for the brain.

Metaphorically, it's a bit like forming a new path through the woods. At first there is no established path, and it takes considerable attention and energy to place your feet in the exact right place to create a path. Then, every day, week, and month that you take this same path, it gets deeper and wider until it eventually requires hardly any energy and conscious awareness to stay on it. It is the same with the brain. As these neuropathways become stronger, the brain begins to prefer them, which is much more efficient for the brain and conserves energy. Neuroscientists refer to this process of developing neuropathways as Hebb's law, whereby "neurons that fire together, wire together."[45] Once the neuropathways are well established, they become unconscious, quick and efficient for the brain.

Neuropathways are the brain's foundation for building more and more complex maps as we interact with the world. The human brain is estimated to have 100 billion neurons, and creates trillions of connections.[46] As we grow and learn, these complex neural maps continually build even more complex neuropathways that act as maps, upon maps, upon maps. This is extremely efficient for the brain because whenever we see something new, think a new thought, or act in a new way, the brain looks for already existing sets of maps to connect it to. Conserving energy through neuropathways has an important upside: they give us a brain that automatically converts our repeated behaviors and attitudes into unconscious habits that save energy and make our lives easier. We don't have to spend valuable energy relearning all of our regular activities: how to brush our teeth, drive to work, respond in routine conversations, send an email, talk to children differently than adults, and so forth. A good example of the degree to which we can rely on these unconscious habits involves the odd experience of driving home from somewhere you go frequently, such as work or the grocery store, and later suddenly realizing you have absolutely no memory of the drive home. And yet, all the time you were driving, you made life and death decisions with no conscious awareness of yourself doing so.

Operating in ways that favor speed and efficiency and favoring what it already knows has some significant benefits for the brain as we have seen, but also poses the significant challenge of automatically and incorrectly ascribing characteristics from our past associations to situations in the present, such as seeing "yellow" ears of corn where there were none. Moreover, these unconscious habits directly affect our ability to consciously and consistently access and operate from the higher brain. This tendency of the brain to rely on unconscious habits and how this impacts the higher brain is considered in great detail by Dr. Kahneman through his study of what he calls "heuristics" and their impact our unconscious thinking, feeling and behaving.

Heuristics

Dr. Daniel Kahneman, winner of the 2002 Nobel Memorial Prize in Economic Sciences and a leader in the study of cognitive bias, provides a helpful way to understand the unconscious brain's influences on the higher brain, and what we can do to engage the higher brain. In his bestselling book, "Thinking Fast and Slow," Dr. Kahneman demonstrates through hundreds of studies that people are much more inclined to let their unconscious brain – what he calls System 1 thinking – run the show than they are to put forth the extra energy and effort needed to consciously engage the reason-based capabilities of the higher brain – what he calls System 2 thinking.

Dr. Kahneman proposes that the brain constantly switches between these two different modes of thought. System 1, the unconscious brain, is fast and instinctive, and operates automatically and effortlessly outside of our conscious awareness. System 2, the higher brain, on the other hand is slow, deliberate, requires more effort, and is used less frequently. A simple math example illustrates these differences. If we are asked to add 2 plus 2, the number 4 comes to us effortlessly – that is System 1 working. We did not have to compute it or do anything deliberately. On the other hand, if someone asks us to multiply 17 times 24, we'd have to invest intentional effort and energy to come up with the correct answer. In this simple example we can see that engaging System 2 requires additional effort. System 2 also represents the reasoning self that is aware of beliefs, makes choices, and consciously decides what to think about and what to do. Dr. Kahneman's extensive experiments in behavioral economics consistently show that while most people believe System 2 is running the show, System 1 is actually more influential. More often than not, System I's impressions and feelings act as the main data source for what seems like our reasoned, conscious choices.[47]

In considering the brain's need for speed and efficiency, Dr. Kahneman describes how System I and the unconscious brain operate on "heuristics." Essentially heuristics are general operating rules – mental shortcuts – that the brain uses to simplify complexity when making decisions, assessments and solving problems. These mental shortcuts conserve brain energy, and allow us to make educated guesses, rely on general rules or principles, and trust our gut instincts. These brain shortcuts are based on trillions of unconsciously associated ideas, beliefs, actions, emotions, and experiences in the brain, and allow us to apply learning from previous experiences to new situations while also conserving brain energy. Heuristics are essential in being able to achieve mastery of a task, and they play a key role in our ability to use hunches and intuition effectively.

On the downside, these mental short cuts and unconscious guidelines can result in faulty connections and incorrect assessments and conclusions. Unconsciously relying on general guidelines and rules causes us to consider only a few aspects of a situation or decision while ignoring other relevant information. In fact, Kahneman describes system 2, or the higher brain, as being "lazy" as evidenced by its "distinct reluctance to invest more effort than is strictly necessary."[48] In fact, when it comes to decision making, neuroscientists estimate that 40 to 60 percent of the decisions we make are unconscious. Overestimating our rational, logical selves while unconsciously defaulting to System I thinking and heuristics has the added effect of creating cognitive biases. More than 175 different types of cognitive biases have been identified by neuroscientists and psychologists, and brain science is now showing the role of the unconscious brain in how they operate. Some of the common ones related to inclusion are provided on the following page.

The Conformation Bias: The tendency to search for, interpret, favor, and recall information in a way that confirms one's preexisting beliefs or hypotheses, while giving disproportionately less consideration to, or ignoring information that challenges our preconceived notions.

The Hindsight Bias: The inclination to see events that have already taken place as being more predictable than they were before they took place.

The Mere Exposure Effect: People tend to develop a preference for things merely because they are familiar. The more exposure we have to a stimulus the more we will tend to like it, even unconsciously.

The Truth Illusion: As we are exposed to a message again and again, it becomes more familiar. Because of the way our minds work, what is familiar seems true. Familiar things require less effort to process and that feeling of cognitive ease signals truth.

The Outcome Bias: A tendency to judge a past decision by its ultimate outcome instead of based on the quality of the decision at the time it was made, given what was known at the time.

The Focusing Illusion: When people place too much importance on one aspect of an event, causing an error in accurately predicting the utility of a future outcome.

The Above-Average Effect: The tendency of people to evaluate themselves more positively than they evaluate most other people.

The Halo Effect: A tendency to use one trait of a person or thing to make an overall judgment of that person or thing. We judge specific traits positively, such as where someone went to school, and use that to make an overall judgment about their performance that is also positive.

The Framing Effect: A cognitive bias in which people react differently to a particular choice depending on whether it is presented as a loss or a gain.

The Priming Effect: Priming is an implicit memory effect in which exposure to a stimulus influences a response to a later stimulus. Your actions and your emotions can be primed by events of which you are not even aware.

The Anchoring Effect: The misconception that you rationally analyze all factors before making a choice or determining value. However, the truth is that your first perception lingers in your mind, affecting later perceptions and decisions.

The Certainty Effect: People tend to select the safer of two prospects, even though it may not be the most rewarding, if this ensures a good outcome with certainty.

The Narrative Fallacy: In a sequential recount of events, a person is inclined to assume that one event within this "narrative" was caused by the previously described events.

Thinking Fast and Slow

In addition to creating cognitive biases, the unconscious brain's reliance on mental shortcuts and operating guidelines creates and supports stereotypical thinking. The unconscious brain matches and links things together in ways that would not make sense to the conscious brain. For example, consider the stereotype that old people "all drive very slowly." We may have that idea from life experiences or from the messages and images we've accumulated over the years, and the unconscious is very happy with that – it's a quick, easy mental shortcut. The rationale thinking brain knows there can be, and are, older drivers who do drive very fast. However, engaging the higher brain to analyze and correct this faulty assumption takes energy and effort, and the higher, conscious brain easily defaults to a less effortful interpretation, even if it's incorrect. If we do see an older person driving fast, more often than not, the conscious brain sees the older drivers as "outliers" rather than as evidence that could challenge a long held stereotype.

The unconscious brain and System 1 thinking are, according to Kahneman, "extremely adept at finding a coherent casual story that links together the fragments of knowledge at its disposal."[49] These mental shortcuts directly translate to behaviors which are often discriminatory, and remain completely out of our awareness. When these unconscious patterns, maps and general operating rules are physically embedded in the brain through neuropathways, it contributes to the difficulty of understanding each other's different worlds across differences. The following situation highlights these difficulties.

Sheila, a female attorney, was hired by a law firm. Once on board, Shelia volunteered to be on the selection committee for hiring more diverse attorneys. As Sheila became more involved in the firm's hiring discussions and decisions, however, she began to notice a disconcerting pattern. Regardless of how strong a female candidates' credentials and qualifications were, the women were subjected to additional scrutiny based on the sole characteristic of whether or not they were "aggressive" enough.

Sheila found this frustrating and unacceptable, and worked hard to convince her colleagues that this approach was actually hurting the firm.

Sheila pointed out that by overweighting this one characteristic of not being aggressive enough, they were actually preventing themselves from considering and hiring the most qualified candidates. She consistently argued that the characteristic of being aggressive was not the sole requirement for being a successful attorney, and referred to her own and other females' non-aggressive yet successful track records as proof. Eventually Sheila earned the label of not being "a team player." At that point Sheila realized that reason and logic would never hold sway against their strong beliefs, and she left the firm.

In this situation, the fact that women leave the firm more quickly and more often than men is not disputed. However, the men and women come to completely different conclusions based on this very same fact. These different interpretations of the facts make resolving the situation very complicated and challenging. It is difficult to find common ground when our different life experiences and beliefs cause completely different interpretations of the very same facts, and these different interpretations result from deeply embedded maps upon maps in our brains about what is normal and most true. The firm's organizational culture clearly primed and reinforced behaviors that normalized a belief about style, meaning that to be successful in the firm one had to be aggressive. The impact of these beliefs and behaviors and the negative consequences of losing talented female attorneys and opening themselves to a lawsuit were not enough to break through to the conscious mind. The priming in the environment and the messages around style were such deeply embedded heuristics that these impacts couldn't be seen or taken into account.

Moving Forward Differently: Neuroscience of Appreciation

We have seen how the unconscious brain conceals the depth of our patterned and biased ways of looking at the world, and a new approach is needed. An approach that helps us engage System 2 thinking to gain more awareness about our biases and keeps the higher brain online so we can make more conscious choices that move us *towards* people who are different from us in ways that build understanding and trust. This new approach is based on the neuroscience of appreciation.

In the past ten years, there has been an increasing number of studies on appreciation and other positive emotions. These findings support what we know intuitively: that positive feelings promote good energy, generosity of spirit, and help us in enjoying our lives. These studies also show that positive feelings such as care, compassion, empathy and joy aid in creating more inclusive workplaces. Neuroscience findings on appreciation clearly show that practicing appreciation-based tools and strategies have a positive impact on both the micro-messages in the work environment and also support the brain establishing new unconscious patterns, norms and assumptions that promote inclusive attitudes and behaviors. A number of these findings on appreciation are instrumental in building our capacity for inclusion. In particular, the findings listed below are especially impactful.

Stabilize the Higher Brain

Positive emotions and appreciation help the higher brain stay online. When positive emotions – both in thoughts and feelings – are engaged, studies show they stabilize the prefrontal cortex.[50] This significantly helps the neocortex do its job in being able to notice and manage assumptions and biases, override discomfort and access our best thinking. This also makes it easier for the brain to engage across differences, even ones that cause us discomfort, and increases our ability to listen outside of what we already know.

Improve Cognitive Functioning

Studies show that positive emotions expand focus and concentration, and are involved in creative thinking, cognitive flexibility, and the processing of information. Positive emotions increase attention and broaden thinking, and cause us to consider and pursue a wider than usual range of precepts and ideas.[51] This increases the brain's ability to understand and hold multiple perspectives, even if they are very different from our own experiences or perspectives.

Increase Empathy and Compassion

In conjunction with the social brain, neuroscience findings now show that positive emotions are tied to our ability to feel compassion and empathy, and involve a set of circuitry in the brain called "mirror neurons." Mirror neurons simulate in our own brains the feelings, actions, and intentions of others, and support our ability to both show empathy to others and experience receiving empathy from others.[52] When positive emotions are engaged, it becomes easier for the brain to extend compassion, cooperation, and appreciation to those who are different from ourselves, strengthening the circuitry of the social brain across differences in the process.

Support High Levels of Motivation and Engagement

Neuroscience studies show that positive emotions can trigger the "reward" pathways located deep within the brain, including in an area known as the ventral striatum – the brain's reward circuitry.[53] When the brain's reward center is activated it produces hormones and chemicals such as dopamine, which keep us motivated and engaged, and able to overcome obstacles and setbacks in achieving our goals.[54] Positive emotions support keeping the reward center online.

Cause an Upward Spiral / Build Personal Resiliency

Positive emotions trigger upward spirals toward enhanced emotional well-being. Put differently, any positive emotion you experience today not only feels good now, but also increases the likelihood you will feel good in the future. Studies that track the same individuals over time have documented that positive emotions and the broadened thinking they bring also lead to reinforcing and sustaining positive mental states and well-being over time.[55]

Are Particularly Contagious

Research is validating that our emotions influence the emotions of those around us. When we are in a positive emotional state, it helps others be in more positive emotional states. Studies also show that people are more likely to help others when they are feeling positive emotions themselves.[56] Good deeds not only spring from positive emotions, they also produce feelings of gratitude and sense of pride in those doing the good deeds.

Can Be Self-generated

Many people believe that in order to feel positive emotions there has to be a good reason, that something good has to happen first. From a brain perspective this simply isn't true. The brain can learn to shift and engage more positive emotional states through intentionally cultivating positive emotions.[57] An example is a recent study that demonstrated it is possible to train brain patterns associated with empathic feelings; more specifically, tenderness. The research showed that volunteers who received neurofeedback about their own brain activity patterns whilst being scanned inside an fMRI machine were able to change brain network function of areas related to tenderness and affection felt toward loved ones at will.[58]

These findings show there is tremendous benefit in consciously engaging positive emotions. We can leverage the neuroscience of appreciation very intentionally to create more inclusive work environments that also support high levels of motivation, innovation and engagement. Cultivating appreciation also supports environments that are characterized by high trust and psychological safety, both of which are essential for inclusion. According to psychologists, psychologically safe environments are emotionally safe and are "characterized by people who feel appreciated, and accepted and able to bring their full selves to their jobs without fear of damage to self-image, status or career."[59]

Psychological safety is a hallmark of inclusive work environments and teams, and has a positive impact on performance. For example, a recently published study by Google found that a salient and differentiating factor between teams that consistently met their goals versus teams that didn't was the successful teams' higher degree of psychological safety. In this study, researchers identified five factors essential for team success: psychological safety, dependability, structure/clarity, meaning of work, and impact of work. Of these factors, psychological safety was determined to be the most salient and consistently reliable factor across all successful teams.[60]

Psychological safety is something that can be intentionally cultivated to help build more inclusive work environments. Based on the latest findings on positive emotions, we are learning that it is possible to create psychologically safe environments by intentionally priming the environment with positive appreciation-based messages, cues and behaviors. In terms of inclusion, creating appreciation-based environments directly supports psychological safety and helps people feel that it is ok to comfortably share who they are, and say what they feel and think without fear of recrimination.

Our new approach to inclusion involves leveraging findings from neuroscience on the power of appreciation to intentionally create work environments that are positive, psychologically safe, and where people feel included, valued, and motivated to do their best work.

Appreciation-Based Tools and Strategies: Building Positive Inclusive Environments

In our new approach there are three appreciation-based strategies and tools designed to positively prime the work environment, and support the brain in building new neuropathways to sustain long-term, positive inclusion behaviors and habits. These strategies help keep the higher brain and System 2 thinking online, and increase our awareness and ability to notice and manage biases. Additionally, these strategies keep the brain tipped towards open-mindedness and curiosity, directly supporting the ability to engage with others across differences and act more inclusively. The three strategies are:

Strategy 1: Build Strong Habits of Appreciation

- Get Good at Compliments
- Cultivate and Model the Emotions You Want Others to Have

Strategy 2: Make Unfamiliar Differences More Familiar

- Meet the Person, Not the Stereotype or Assumption in Your Head
- Use Storytelling and Find Connections

Strategy 3: Make Expectations Positive and Explicit

- Hold and Communicate High Expectations
- Expand Your "Go To" People

Strategy 1: Build Strong Habits of Appreciation

Building strong habits of appreciation is imperative for creating positive work environments. Research shows that the brain has a strong negativity bias, and hangs onto negative messages much more strongly than it does to positive ones. It is generally agreed that it takes anywhere from 7-10 positive messages to undo one negative message. Anyone who has fretted the entire weekend over a last minute negative comment from your boss knows how this works. Suddenly your good mood shifts to fear and doubt, and your mind spins with questions like, "What did they mean by that? Am I being sidelined? How secure *is* my job?"

Positive comments are nice to receive and we welcome them, but they don't have the same degree of traction in our system. The brain's negativity bias is often described as velcro for negative experiences and teflon for positive ones. If someone gives us a positive compliment as we're leaving work, we feel good, until 5 minutes later when someone cuts us off in traffic and we get angry. Positive emotions are essential to inclusion, higher cognitive functioning, and enhanced performance, yet they are softer and more easily displaced than negative emotions. When environments are fear based, or there is a lot of pressure, stress and urgency, it is much more difficult to engage and sustain positive emotions. To keep positive emotions online and have more positive behaviors and positive cues in the environment, we need to be very intentional in strengthening the neuropathways of positive emotions. The following practices help us prime positive, more inclusive behaviors and attitudes in the work environment, making it easier to engage and sustain positive emotions.

Get Good at Compliments

In the workplace, positive emotions and behaviors directly impact our brain's reward center, which is directly involved in the circuitry underlying motivation and engagement. It is essential to employee engagement and empowerment to make it a regular practice to give compliments, appreciation and microaffirmations that tell individuals they are welcome, visible, valued, and capable of performing with the same level of resources and expectations as everyone else.

Consistently practicing getting good at giving compliments has a powerful effect on inclusion. Even just small gestures such as smiling and saying "thank you" reinforce the brain's reward center and create positive feelings about one's value, importance, and personal contribution. According to some researchers, microaffirmations may even have a more dramatic effect on correcting performance than formal performance reviews. According to Anna Giraldo-Kerr, a Harvard researcher on microinequities and microaffirmations, "tiny acts of appreciation" are more meaningful to employees than performance reviews because they are personal, in the moment, not expected, and best of all, they are sincere. [61]

There are a multitude of ways we can get good at giving compliments and sending positive messages to others that they are valued, respected and appreciated. Some ways you can do this include:

- Giving someone positive feedback on the spot
- Inviting someone to lunch you don't typically have lunch with
- Offering your assistance
- Ensuring your tone is warm and upbeat

- Referring positively to the work of a person to others
- Making a positive introduction of someone to others
- Telling someone why you liked what they did and the positive impact it had
- Asking for someone's input or advice
- Commenting positively and on someone's unique talents and specific contributions

It only takes an extra few seconds to let someone know you appreciate them and their contributions. For example, stopping what you're doing to listen intently to someone, consciously sending encouraging body language and facial expressions, and smiling and greeting everyone with the same degree of interest and respect, are all examples of small positive behaviors of inclusion. Showing positive gestures and behaviors towards every person equally can become a habit that, when practiced consistently and sincerely, gets established in the brain as an unconscious and automatic response. Just like microinequities, microaffirmations have a cumulative effect on individuals and on the work environment. The unconscious brain is continually scanning and being primed for "how we do things around here," and small positive behaviors that become habits get translated into an organization's culture. When we create a consistent practice and habit of getting good at compliments, we positively prime the people around us and the work environment, creating a more inclusive, motivating and positive environment that also helps keep the prefrontal cortex online, and peoples' ability to consciously override unconscious biases more consistently.

Cultivate and Model the Emotions You Want Others to Have

Neuroscience is showing that through the mirror neuron circuitry in the brain our emotions are contagious. Mirror neurons are involved in the brain's unconscious reading of each other's social cues, and our moods and emotions are actually experienced in the brain's those around us.[62] When we are in a positive emotional state, the associated gestures, feelings and even intentions will be replicated in other peoples' brains. We can intentionally generate positive feelings in ourselves and create contagious positive emotions that have a positive impact on those around us and the work environment.

Make it a practice to periodically throughout the day stop and notice what emotions and thoughts you are modeling. If they are no longer positive, make a conscious choice to re-engage positive emotions. Essentially, we can think about or do anything that creates feeling states that are positive. For instance, here are some ways to cultivate positive emotions:

- Check my tone of voice to make sure it is warm and positive
- Be open to feedback about my word choices and non-verbal behaviors to ensure they are having a positive impact
- Stop every couple of hours and take a moment to focus on something that makes me feel happy
- Create a gratitude list of all the things I am grateful for
- When I am in conversations, think about what I appreciate about the person I am speaking with
- Focus on the good things that are happening around me
- Get good at giving compliments; as I create positive emotions for others it will enhance my own
- Make a habit of sending conscious positive messages to myself
- Take time to do things (i.e. activities, hobbies, time with friends) that bring me joy and happiness

The more we focus on engaging positive emotions, the more we will build and strengthen the associated circuitry and neuropathways in the brain, increasing our capacity to sustain positive emotions in ourselves, while also unconsciously sending positive messages to others and positively priming the work environment.[63]

Strategy 2: Make Unfamiliar Differences More Familiar

Another strategy to positively influence the work environment and make it easier for the brain to engage across differences is to actively work to make unfamiliar differences more familiar in positive, non-threatening ways. We now know just being in a diverse environment is not enough to be inclusive and we need to go beyond this and engage in authentic, meaningful relationships across differences. The research is clear that actively engaging across differences in ways that are positive and authentic is what improves understanding and builds trust.[64] Additionally, research on reversing the effect of racial bias in children and other studies show how "familiarizing the unfamiliar" is a positive and powerful way to reduce unconscious bias. Studies show that negative racial biases and stereotypes cannot be reduced by logic and reason alone; however, they can definitely be reduced and even re-patterned by positive interactions and exposure to more positive images in the media.[65]

When we build connections and relationships across differences, we create positive associations in the brain which primes the brain to see someone's difference in a more positive light, and it increases our ability to regard them as an "us." When a difference becomes familiar and positive and more "normalized," it creates a sense of cognitive ease in the brain, making it easier for the social brain to engage, and for us to extend care, compassion and kindness across differences. When we work to make differences more familiar and build our understanding and comfort, it makes it easier for us to regard each other with more open-mindedness, and engage in conversations that lead to a recognition of shared interests, needs, and outcomes.

Meet the Person, Not the Stereotype or Assumption in Your Head

We have seen how part of the job of the unconscious brain is to fill in the gaps and connect fragments of impressions and data into a believable story. When we meet people, our brains automatically create stories about who they are, often under the radar of our conscious awareness. It only takes the brain milliseconds to determine whether someone shows up as an "us" or a "them" based on race, gender, body language, attire, facial expressions, height, weight, attractiveness, etc.. The brain unconsciously responds to thousands of different cues, and puts people in categories and constructs a narrative that may have nothing to do with who the person standing in front of us really is.

In learning to recognize and manage unconscious biases, it is very helpful to understand that the brain makes up stories about people, and we don't have to believe them. We can learn to notice how quickly the stories show up based on past experiences and other messages, and then consciously set them aside. We can then make connections with the actual person in front of us and choose to:

- Be curious and willing to learn more about who the individual really is
- Look for and notice information that does not fit our preconceived ideas
- Shape a new, positive narrative that is based on new things we find out about someone that we can appreciate or respect

We can learn to set aside our assumptions by recognizing that they are just that – assumptions – and meet people with an open mind and find out who they really are. We can consciously replace misinformation with a new, positive narrative that will aid us in working together more effectively.

Use Storytelling and Find Connections

We know how quickly the brain creates narratives based on stereotypes and faulty assumptions, and how these get in the way of being inclusive. Intentional storytelling, on the other hand, is a way to listen openly to each other's real stories and experiences, and a powerful way to create shared understanding, connections and resonance with others. When we are being told a story, not only are the language processing parts in our brain activated, but other areas including the emotion area and the motor resonance area also become engaged. Furthermore, the brain of the person telling a story and the brain of the person listening to it can synchronize,[66] further fueling an experience of resonance.

When we tell stories and listen to other people's stories, we build connections across differences and find similar likes or dislikes, experiences, or interests that we otherwise would not have known. From a brain perspective, building connections builds familiarity and comfort for the brain and keeps the reward center online. Through stories we share our common human experiences. The details of our lives may differ greatly, yet we can all appreciate and identify with the feelings, reactions, needs and aspirations of each other's lives. Sharing stories also helps us notice our implicit biases and assumptions, as well as the unconscious brain's reactions to differences. Hearing each other's stories helps shift the brain from seeing someone who is different as an "other" to being seen as part of "us." Telling stories can also make it easier to talk about aspects of differences or challenges that may arise.

Both individuals and organizations can look for and create opportunities to share stories and build connections. As an individual, you can seek out people you typically don't go to lunch or have coffee with and intentionally enjoy a conversation that is not just focused on work, but also includes topics that build connections, such as hobbies, movies, music, different places you've visited, and so forth. In organizations, storytelling can be used as a specific strategy for integrating and building trust among a highly diverse work group. For example, one particular organization made storytelling an on-going practice. At regularly scheduled staff meetings, different individuals volunteered to tell their "story." They were given 10 minutes to show photos and any objects they wanted to tell about themselves – where they've come from, what matters to them, challenges and blessings they have received and the things that shaped them to become who they are today. As the person told their story, people experienced a much fuller sense of who that person really is and were able to make connections and resonate with similar feelings and experiences. As new employees joined the organization, they also shared their stories which quickly built a sense of connection and trust with other employees and the organization, changed how people interacted with them in very positive ways, and further primed the environment for behaviors of inclusion.

Strategy 3: Make Expectations Positive and Explicit

A number of psychological studies have demonstrated that high expectations directly boost performance while low expectations, even unconscious ones, have a detrimental impact on performance.[67] Claude Steele, Stanford University, and Joshua Aronson, University of Texas, have been studying the impact of "stereotype threat" on expectations and performance for many years. The term "stereotype threat" refers to an internalized sense that one might be judged in terms of negative stereotypes about one's group instead of being judged on their personal merits. Steele and Aronson's research on stereotype threat has found that being part of a historically discriminated group and the internally associated negative stereotypes, assumptions and low expectations is enough to negatively impact performance. Remarkably, their research also shows that by making unconscious expectations explicit, it can positively prime the brain for success. Consider the following two studies.

One study involved two different groups of students, and both groups were comprised of black and white students. The students in both groups were given a test comprised of 20 questions from the GRE (Graduate Record Examination). In Group 1, the white and black students scored equally well. In Group 2, the students were given an additional instruction on the pretest questionnaire, and were asked to mark a box indicating their race. This priming proved to be a powerful impact on performance as the number of correct answers among black students in Group 2 dropped significantly. When the researchers talked to the black students after the test and asked them if anything lowered their performance, or if it bothered them that they were asked to indicate their race, the majority of students said "no." Yet, the African-American students who were asked to answer the question about their racial background performed markedly less well than their African-American peers who were not asked to identify their race.

Later, the researchers decided to test the reverse and prime students to believe that race would not impact their performance. In this study, the researchers told the African American students explicitly that checking the race box has had no impact on performance results, and emphasized that everyone can perform well on the test regardless of their race. This simple, explicit statement turned out to be very powerful. The black students performed equivalently with their white peers. The results showed that performance is influenced greatly by the cues in the environment. When the cues are intentionally positive – or at the very least neutralized – performance improves.

Additional studies show that other dimensions of difference can also be vulnerable to stereotype threat and have a negative impact on performance. For example, studies done with women on math tests, Latinos on verbal tests, and elderly individuals (who face the stereotype about poor memory) on tests of short-term memory, show that these stereotypes can become internally associated and reduce performance.[68] Whether we are in a social group that is subject to stereotype threat or not, these findings expose the power of other people's expectations on our internal expectations of ourselves and how this carries forward into our performance. Making unconscious expectations positive and explicit is a powerful way to impact people's self-expectations and help them boost their performance.

Hold and Communicate High Expectations

As individuals, we can consciously hold and explicitly communicate high expectations to create a climate of success within organizations. We can positively prime other people's brains for success by voicing our belief in them that they are capable of success, and reinforce positive messages that show we assume they will be successful. For instance, one elementary school with predominately students of color has worked creatively to break the cycle of low expectations and low high school graduation rates in their area. Each classroom in the school is named after a different college, and the teachers and staff consciously prime the students with messages that set explicit positive expectations of being successful students, graduating from high school and earning college degrees. This approach, along with other efforts of the Northside Achievement Zone, uses the power of explicit, positive expectations to propel student success.[69]

In organizations, a highly effective way to make unconscious expectations explicit is to share the unwritten rules for success. This can be done in a variety of ways, from formal mentoring programs that explicitly include the unwritten rules for success, to employee resource and network groups, to a seasoned employee sharing them with a new employee. Another way to hold and communicate high expectations is to ask the people you work with what they need from you to feel supported and successful in their work. Everyone can work to make unconscious expectations explicit and positive to build a culture of success.

Expand Your "Go To" People

It is commonplace within organizations that leaders can develop unconscious habits of who becomes their preferred "go to" people that they rely on, give high visibility opportunities to and groom for success. We've seen the brain's inherent bias towards people it perceives to be similar and more like an "us." This tendency is not easy to overcome, but recognizing that it exists as a fact of the brain's wiring and unconscious tendencies, is an essential first step. Start paying close attention to the individuals you automatically expect to do well, and that you easily and comfortably give opportunities to stretch and grow. Learn to recognize and challenge this brain bias by consciously extending the same opportunities, support and resources to all members of the team. It's also important to remember that team members are easily primed to treat other team members with the same attitudes and behaviors that the leader does. Team members can develop unconscious expectations and habits of who they go to for help and assistance on their team and who they do not. These unconscious habits creates stagnation and low expectations among those who also would benefit from development opportunities and coaching to grow and become future leaders.

Check your own habits of who are your "go to" people. Make a list of all the people you work with regularly, then note the specific individuals on the list that tend to be your "go to" people. Look at the range of diversity among this "go to" group and see what patterns you notice. The brain's "us" bias and preference for comfort, efficiency and ease can greatly influence who we see as potential stars. Ask yourself why they are your "go to" people. Perhaps their work style, background or education is similar to yours, making it easier for you to connect and understand each other. Next, evaluate your own expectations of the people that are not on your "go to" list. How can you consciously expand that circle of "go to" people, and hold and communicate high expectations of others and expect them to also deliver and succeed?

To consciously expand your "go to" people, you can:

- Ask yourself what you can do differently to create positive high expectations for those who are not currently your "go to" people.
- Reflect on the performance of each person on your team. Ask yourself how their performance could be related to your biases – positive or negative.
- Consider any performance issues or concerns on your team. What are your unconscious expectations about those team members? If there are low expectations, how might these be impacting their performance? How can you shift that?

Summary

We now see how we can choose to positively prime the work environment through the neuroscience of appreciation. By intentionally sending messages that let people know they matter in big and small ways, we can create work environments that feel supportive, are psychologically safe, and where people are motivated to perform at their highest levels, take risks, and bring their full self to work. When people routinely practice these kinds of positive affirming behaviors, these messages and behaviors get embedded into the organization's unconscious way of doing business. To do this however, also involves understanding and being able to override the tendencies of the defensive brain. The defensive brain, just like the unconscious brain, can interfere with our good intentions to be inclusive and, in particular, make communicating across differences extremely challenging. The good news is that in understanding the defensive brain, we can target and override defensive communication patterns, and build trust by learning to listen outside of what we already know, thereby deepening our understanding of others' different experiences and world views to work together more effectively.

CHAPTER THREE

S.A.V.E. Communications: Outsmarting the Defensive Brain

"I've learned that people will forget what you said, people will forget what you did, but people will never forget how you made them feel."
-Maya Angelou

Did you know that every single person's brain is built on the defensive? It is true. Deep within each of our brains is a survival-based threat response that is still very much with us today. Our brains are spring loaded to protect and defend us against possible threats. Dr. Edward Hallowell, a psychiatrist and founder of the Hallowell Center for Cognitive and Emotional Health, states: "There may not be lions or bears roaming the halls of your organization, but people's brains are oriented to perceive threats."[70] The brain does not differentiate between threats to our physical safety and threats to our social need for inclusion and respect by our peers. Microinequities and other messages of exclusion and marginalization are all threats to the brain's survival-based need for social belonging.

The threat response can easily get triggered in communication with others, especially across differences. When triggered, it narrows our perceptual field and diminishes our ability to see options, consider others' points of view, while it also undermines our capacity to see and understand the consequences of our behavior. When the threat response creates a narrowing of perception, it generates a number of brain dynamics that easily lead to misunderstandings, judgments, negative assumptions, and an inability to find common ground. When these dynamics go unmanaged, they result in a downward spiral of escalating conflicts. To communicate in ways that develop understanding and build trust across differences means learning to effectively manage the threat response, which involves first understanding how it works.

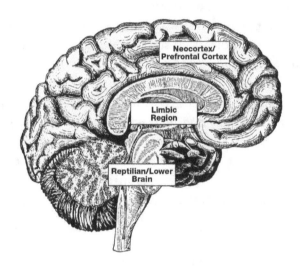

The oldest part of the brain, often referred to as the "reptilian brain" or "lower brain," is tied directly to our survival circuitry and is actively scanning for threats in the environment 24/7, both physical and psychological. The threat response is wired much more strongly in the brain than the brain's social wiring for empathy and collaboration. It also comes on more quickly and its effects stay longer. The lower brain is most directly connected with the body's nervous system, and when triggered it exerts tremendous influence on our thoughts, emotions, and physical bodies. The threat response sends the brain into a strong defense mode (fight, flight, or freeze), and the brain immediately shifts into defending and protecting one's self, often outside of our conscious awareness. One of the most important aspects of the threat response is that when it gets triggered, it destabilizes the prefrontal cortex, and takes the higher brain offline.

Every day in the workplace, our brains are actively scanning for possible threats. One minute we can be engaged in a very productive team conversation with lots of collaboration and joint problem solving going on, and then someone says something, and the threat response gets triggered, and everyone's brains start to derail. We saw this happen in a client situation recently. A task force was making their recommendations to the rest of the team, and this included summarizing the costs involved in making a much needed upgrade to one of their technical processes. In the meeting, the person presenting the recommendation said, "To do all of the parts of the upgrade process at once would cost $500,000, but we're recommending doing it in stages." Nobody heard the last part of the sentence: "to do it in stages." The number $500,000 triggered such a strong threat response among the team members that the meeting went downhill, and caused divisiveness within the team based on who was "for" spending the money and who was "against" spending the money. The conversation about what would be needed to update the system, and how much it would cost in stages never occurred, and the upgrade never happened. When the threat response gets triggered, and goes unmanaged, it negatively impacts productivity, motivation, and engagement as well as long-term relationships. Consider the following situation.

Randall and Jeffrey are leaders in a large consumer food organization. Jeffrey is head of Research & Development, and Randall leads the Marketing Department. For the past six months, they have been working together on a joint project, and the final status meeting with their senior leadership team is scheduled for the next day. In preparing for the meeting, they decided that Jeffrey would go first.

The morning of the meeting, Jeffrey texted Randall to let him know he was running a few minutes late. Jeffrey didn't hear back from Randall right away, but he wasn't concerned as meetings often started five minutes late. When Jeffrey arrived, however, he was surprised to find that not only had the meeting started, but Randall was fully engaged in presenting his marketing campaign to the group. Jeffrey noticed that the senior leaders, including the CEO, were all highly engaged, asking lots of questions and complimenting Randall on his work.

Confused and ticked off, Jeffrey didn't understand Randall's decision to begin without him. At the half-way mark, Randall was still responding to questions, and Jeffrey decided to cut in on him. That went okay, but now Jeffrey was rushed and also found it hard to keep the senior leaders' attention. There had been so much energy in the room when he first walked in, and now he sensed there was less interest and enthusiasm about the product development process and how well it was going. Nevertheless, he finished his main points, and there were a few good questions at the end. Jeffrey felt he had done a good job. He also thought that if he had gone first like they planned, he would have been able to create more engagement and recognition for his work.

After the meeting, Randall and Jeffrey were in very different places. Randall was thrilled and felt triumphant while Jeffrey felt angry, frustrated and intentionally maligned. Jeffrey was sure that Randall had tried to upstage him by going first, and had taken advantage of his being a few minutes late. Walking right up to Randall, Jeffrey said, "What are you doing? We agreed that I would go first!" Randall was taken aback, and said, "Hey calm down. I started the meeting before you arrived because Tom (their boss) asked me to. I meant to text you, but it happened really fast." Jeffrey ignored this comment, and said, "I am really sick of you grandstanding in front of this group!" At that point, Jeffrey walked away and resolved to never trust Randall again.

In this situation, Jeffrey's defensive brain came on so strong that he was not able to hear Randall's explanation that their boss had asked him to start first. Jeffrey's unmanaged threat response prevented him from learning the truth that Randall had no intention of upstaging him, and was simply asked by their boss to go first. Instead, Jeffrey's threat-based response caused him to make an incorrect interpretation of the events, and then further, to make a decision based on a limited view of what actually happened - a decision that will have lasting consequences.

Understanding the dynamics of the threat response is crucial to learning to communicate more effectively when working across differences. A very important aspect of the threat response is that it impacts our level of perception. It turns out that perception is not static in the brain, and when the threat response is triggered, it dramatically reduces our ability to access and see the bigger picture. It then becomes very challenging to try to understand someone else's different experience or perspective. In the situation above, we don't know the backgrounds of Jeffrey and Randall, but it is easy to imagine that if either of them had biases about the others' differences, it could easily lead to further incorrect interpretations and conclusions. For example, consider the exact same situation but imagine that Randall is a white male and Jeffrey is a black female. Do you notice any additional stories or assumptions that arise in your brain as you consider the situation? Or, consider Randall, and what if he is a white female in her 60s and Jeffrey is a white male in his 20s? How does this affect your assumptions and interpretations? Or what if Jeffrey is in a wheel chair? Or if one of them is transgender?

We can see that when we add in differences to the situation, various stories, stereotypes and assumptions get added in to the dynamics of the conversation. Even when these are outside of our awareness, they can still directly influence the way we interpret what's going on, and the conclusions we make about the individuals involved. When the threat response is triggered and there are differences involved, it is also easy for the brain to consider someone's differences as the only relevant factors involved in the conflict. When access to the higher brain and the bigger picture are offline, the assumptions, stories and stereotypes we have about someone's differences easily get confirmed rather than challenged. This makes it even more difficult to notice and challenge our biases because they can start to feel like "proof" that our assumptions are the truth, and that we are justified in having them. With the narrowing of perception in the brain, it doesn't naturally occur to us to challenge our assumptions, and turn the tables to look at the situation from the other person's perspective - even though that is exactly what we need to do.

The Neuroscience of Perception and the Downward Spiral

From a survival perspective, narrowing our perceptual field serves the purpose of helping the brain focus on only what is needed in that moment. However, when the threat response is triggered in communicating with others, and perceptual narrowing kicks in, we lose the ability to see the world through the eyes of others, and really listen beyond our already preconceived ideas and assumptions. It makes it challenging to really hear what someone else is saying. For example, this dynamic can get in the way of individuals giving and receiving feedback, especially when the feedback to someone is about a microinequity they are exhibiting. A recent situation demonstrates how feedback that is intended to be helpful, and is important for someone to talk about, can trigger a threat response in the other person, and if not managed well, can cause a narrowing of perception and a downward spiral in communication.

Kirk, who is deaf, asked his co-worker Roseanne to make a small change in her behavior. Kirk explained that when he brings a signer with him to large meetings, he would like Roseanne to look at him rather than at the signer when she is talking to him. Roseanne's response was, "sure, no problem." Later, Kirk found out that Roseanne was making disparaging remarks about his "special needs." When Kirk confronted her about her derogatory statements, she laughed and told him to "lighten up" and that it was just a joke. In that moment, Kirk's threat response was triggered, and in strong words he told her she was wrong to be making jokes about this. His strong reaction triggered a defensive reaction in Roseanne, and she felt Kirk was now demonstrating her point, that he was definitely overly sensitive. She told him he needed to remember that being a professional does not include being a complainer. The conversation ended abruptly with each person believing strongly that they were right in their perception of the situation. Kirk concluded that Roseanne has biases against deaf people and is going to be difficult to work with going forward, and Rosanne concluded that Kirk is overly sensitive. If they both understood the dynamics of the threat response and the narrowing of perception, they could work to bring the prefrontal cortex back online, reconsider their assumptions about each other, and resolve the situation more effectively.

A downward spiral of reacting to each other's reactions in communication is a common occurrence in challenging and difficult conversations, especially across differences. It often happens before we have even realized the threat response has been triggered and that we are caught up in a negative reaction. When the threat response is not noticed or managed effectively, it is easy to say or do things that trigger the threat response in the other person, and when this happens it is very easy for the conversation to spiral downward into a back and forth triggering of negative reactions in each other. In this downward spiral, effective communication and dialogue are blocked, and opportunities for learning, insight, and self-reflection are lost. When perception narrows, other dynamics come into play that, if not managed, can add even more fuel to the downward spiral.

Increased Confidence You Are Right

A dynamic factor in the narrowing of perception is that it increases our confidence, and we feel more certain that our view or interpretation is definitely right.[71] As the threat response increases, and as thinking devolves into ever more "either/or" perceptions, the brain sees fewer perceived options. There is also a corresponding confidence that the "one way" we see it is definitely the most accurate and most true. As perception narrows and we grow more certain that we are right, the thought of shifting from a strong "I" point of view to a "You" or "We" point of view is very counter-intuitive, if not completely illogical to the brain.[72] Why should I step back and consider a different way of looking at this when every bone in my body is telling me that I am right? Our ability to consider another way of looking at a situation can become so paltry and restricted that the only point of view we can tolerate is our own. This is what happened with Kirk and Roseanne, and we also saw it in the situation with Jeffrey and Randall. In both situations, the narrowing of perception and the increasing certainty of being right made individuals unable to consider another point of view.

When the threat response goes unmanaged, it overrides the higher brain and diminishes access to self-awareness, open-mindedness and new choices. When perception narrows, and people can't see anything but their own point of view, no new information can get in. This also undermines our ability to engage the higher brain and maintain sufficient self-awareness to recognize we need to make a new choice. This is a challenging brain dynamic. It turns out that just when we need self-awareness the most, we have the least ability and motivation to access it. The more sure we are right, the less it occurs to us that we need more awareness. This dynamic represents one of the most difficult aspects of learning to manage the threat response. A colleague of ours says, "When I'm sure I'm right, be afraid, be very afraid." In moments of absolute assurance that we are right, we need to train ourselves to know, even though it feels completely counter-intuitive, that a myriad of other options, possibilities and perspectives still exist. Without the ability to understand and override this dynamic, inclusion conversations can slide into a blind alley of downward spirals, confirming our negative assumptions, judgements and stereotypes, while we also lose any opportunity to learn something new. To manage the threat response effectively also involves understanding an area of the brain called the amygdala and its impact on perception.

Low Resolution and the Amygdala

The amygdala plays a key role in the threat response as it can detect and immediately react to perceived threats without having to first go through the brain's decision centers. It is continually scanning the environment on the lookout for threats – physical and psychological – and it is able to process millions of bits of incoming information every second by operating on what is called "low resolution."[73] By operating on low resolution, the brain is constantly prepared to defend itself against possible threats even though it might not have all the relevant information as it does so.

For example, the brain might quickly perceive a snake on the path ahead and trigger a threat response, but as we get closer, we see that it is just a stick and no threat at all.

Low resolution is like a photograph that is being displayed in a thumbnail version. When looking at a thumbnail photograph, we know the entire picture is there, but the specific details are blurred or not even visible. The amygdala operates in a similar way. As it scans our environment for threats, it condenses, subdues, blurs and misses important details that can result in faulty conclusions.

This low resolution effect can also cause the brain to confuse emotional events from the past with events and behaviors in the present. For example, if you have had significant experiences being marginalized or treated as a "less than" in your life, then even a small microinequity, such as your boss not listening with their full attention, or someone mispronouncing your name (again), can trigger a strong emotional reaction that isn't completely related to the present situation. These emotions can come on very strong and very quickly without any awareness of what is driving the reaction. Dr. Srini Pillay refers to this process as memory "zip files" opening in the brain because it releases stored information, emotions, and experiences all at once. When this happens, the brain can become flooded with previous memories and emotions that aren't necessarily related to the current situation or event. This can also cause people who have not experienced marginalization, or thought about it deeply, to judge someone's strong emotional reaction as a character flaw. This can lead to further misperceptions, negative assumptions and breakdowns in trust, and the opportunity to seek to understand and respond with compassion is lost.

Understanding the threat response and its impact on our perception, assumptions, conclusions and behavior is a good thing. It gives us knowledge that we can use to be smarter in communicating with others. We can learn to recognize the signs that it has been triggered, and develop a strong habit of reminding ourselves that during a strong threat response our brains are usually telling us a limited and negative story. It is important and very helpful to develop a solid and unequivocal understanding that the threat response narrows perceptions and causes us to:

- Mistake situations that are not threatening for ones that are threatening (the snake)
- Lose access to self-awareness, open-mindedness and conscious choices (increased confidence we are right)
- Increase defensiveness and negativity (we will protect ourselves and blame external circumstances or others)
- Reinforce stereotypical perspectives and then further conclude that they are true and we are right to have them (no motivation to challenge our assumptions and biases)
- Not see or even believe there are other options available (no access to the higher brain and seeing a broader range of possibilities)
- Misperceive or not even see the specific details of a situation or event (get stuck in arguments of what happened and only see confirming evidence)
- Incorrectly connect events in the present with "seeming similar" strong emotional memories from the past causing strong reactions to what might seem to others like small or incidental events (leads to judgments and misunderstandings)

By understanding these facts, we become more motivated and better able to manage the threat response, preventing the "us vs. them" dynamics from overtaking and dominating our conversations with others. The narrowing of perception can make it seem like defending ourselves or blaming others is justified. In the moment, these perceptions feel very real and need to be handled with care. However, this isn't the only road to go down. In the bigger picture, there are always many other avenues available. It's just that we can't access them in the moment – or sometimes even believe they exist – because the defensive brain limits our thinking, overtakes our physiology and makes our emotions feel like the only truth. We need to understand that the threat response gives us an outdated survival-based view of the world that is based on fear of the unfamiliar. If we don't learn to consciously manage this tendency, especially in our communications with others, we will not be able to shape a more inclusive brain, and develop increasingly better inclusion skills across differences.

We need a new approach to communicating across differences. We need specific communication skills to manage the dynamics of the defensive brain, and at the same time help us leverage the brain's built-in social circuitry for cooperation, connection and compassion, strengthening its capacity to engage across differences. Learning to communicate in ways that strengthen these capacities provides a great opportunity to both stabilize the higher brain and advance our capacity to create conversations where people feel heard, validated, and safe to share who they are and what they really think. This doesn't mean we agree with everyone. It simply means we consciously strengthen the brain's less evolved but fully capable social circuitry to listen outside of what we already know, and focus on what we do share and what connects us, even if it feels counter-intuitive to our base instincts to do so.

Engaging a Care Frame™

Engaging a Care Frame™ is the start point for countering the effects of the threat response in communicating across differences. This first step builds a container of appreciation that helps reduce defensiveness in ourselves and others. Engaging a Care Frame means consciously engaging a feeling of appreciation and positive regard towards another person – or group of people – as we communicate with them. This appreciation-based approach to communicating helps counter the effects of perceptual narrowing and supports the higher brain staying online. With the higher brain online and access to higher level perceptions, we can more effectively listen outside of what we already know. This opens the possibility for more authentic dialogue by creating a genuine conversation that advances our understanding and regard for each other's unique stories, experiences and perspectives.

From neuroscience we know that our individual thoughts, feelings, intentions and behaviors are directly replicated in other peoples' brains through the mirror neuron system.[74] The more we consciously engage a Care Frame in our conversations with others, the more their brains will replicate a positive response within themselves and mirror a positive response back. This is what we call creating an "upward spiral" in communication. By consciously engaging a Care Frame, we assist our mirror neurons in sending positive feelings and signals to others peoples' brains, and this generates an upward spiral of positive messages back and forth. It also creates the opportunity to practice attitudes and behaviors that will build and strengthen the circuitry of the social brain, improving our ability to extend empathy and compassion toward others. We've seen through the neuroscience of appreciation that this also stabilizes the higher brain and keeps it online. This is what makes it possible for us to consciously and intentionally focus on the ways we are connected, look for shared interests, seek to understand and appreciate the ways we are different. This allows us to enhance and advance our communication patterns across differences.

Moreover, an appreciation-based approach to communication is essential for building trust. Neuroscience findings show that an unmanaged threat response takes the brain's reward system off-line. When the reward center is off-line, the brain cannot produce oxytocin, and this creates a serious problem. Oxytocin is the essential brain chemical for building trust, and it must be present in the brain for trust to occur. Sometimes referred to as the "love hormone" or the "moral molecule," oxytocin is released in the brain when we feel cared about, loved and appreciated. Oxytocin is what makes it possible for us to openly move towards others who are different from ourselves and be interested in learning more about them. It is also instrumental in the brain's ability to shift from self-interest to seeing others' interests as important, and is shown to boost group-serving behavior when it is present in the brain.[75]

Engaging a Care Frame brings appreciation online, and with it the brain's reward system and the ability to produce oxytocin. We know that appreciation also helps the higher brain stay online, and as such, Engaging a Care Frame becomes the foundation and baseline capacity for communicating more effectively across differences.

The S.A.V.E. Communication™ Model

There are four specific steps and strategies we can rely on that will help to sustain a Care Frame within ourselves and help reduce defensiveness in others. This new, four step S.A.V.E. Communication™ Model takes place within an intentional Care Frame, and helps us prevent or "save" a conversation from the threat response's defensive and narrow perceptions. These four steps support keeping the higher brain to stay online, while increasing opportunities for understanding and building trust across differences.

S.A.V.E. Communication™ Model

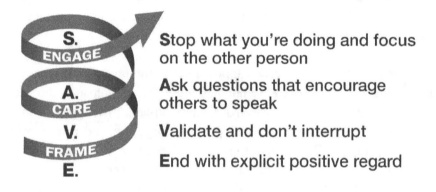

S.
ENGAGE
Stop what you're doing and focus on the other person

A.
CARE
Ask questions that encourage others to speak

V.
FRAME
Validate and don't interrupt

E.
End with explicit positive regard

STEP 1: Stop what you're doing and focus on the other person

Developing the ability to intentionally focus one's attention is essential for advancing inclusive communication skills. Giving someone your undivided attention is a clear demonstration of respect, and it is an action that communicates you value a person's ideas and input. However, in today's world of quickly changing priorities, ongoing demands, and increasing unpredictability, maintaining focus and attention can be very challenging for the brain. A Harvard business review article titled "Overloaded Circuits: Why Smart People Under Perform," coined the term ADD - Adult Digital Disorder, for what they see as an epidemic of poor focus and reduced attention skills among leaders.[76] Our attention is pulled in multiple directions at once every day, and it impacts the messages we send in our interactions with others. Dr. Srini Pillay, author of Your Brain and Business, proposes that a critical leadership skill in the 21st century is "being able to harness and direct attention at will." Others are referring to the skill of focusing attention as "the new currency for leadership success."[77]

Focusing our undivided attention on someone else, and listening with our full attention to their point of view, beliefs, stories and perspectives takes practice. We like to hear ourselves talk. We like to express our own point of view, say what we know and tell others about how the world shows up for us. An interesting study on advice giving underscores this point. Researchers in this study looked at the brain scans of people as they received advice, and also watched the brains of the people who were giving the advice. The researchers discovered that when people were receiving advice, their brains showed very little activity, about the same as passively watching TV. However, the brain scans of the people giving the advice were full of activity. In other words, giving advice is exciting and we like doing it, but it has very little effect on the brains of the people we are giving it to.

When we don't give someone our full attention, it may seem like a small behavior, but it can have an enormous impact. For people who have been marginalized – for whatever reason – and have experienced microinequities on a regular basis, it can feel even more pronounced. It can feel like "here's yet another example of how I'm ignored and people don't feel they have to pay attention to what I have to say." It can trigger a defensive brain reaction, and have the effect of individuals becoming reluctant to engage in future conversations. After all, why would someone want to bring up issues or concerns when they don't feel like they will get people's undivided attention and they won't really get heard? When we don't stop and focus on the other person, it can erode trust very quickly and can even become more evidence fueling an experience of marginalization. When people don't feel heard, they go to lawyers to get heard.

A practical way to develop the skill of focusing our attention on others is to engage a Care Frame. When we stop what we are doing, and consciously extend appreciation and positive regard towards someone, it helps focus our attention. Engaging a Care Frame also strengthens the circuitry of the social brain across differences making the habit easier and more natural over time. When we stop and give someone our undivided attention in communicating across differences, we send a message of respect and that they matter, and we are also less likely to send mixed signals through our own body language and words. Engaging in this simple practice of giving people our undivided attention helps ensure individuals feel valued, respected and heard, significantly improving communication across differences.

Step 2: Ask questions that encourage others to speak

Learning to ask good questions that encourage others to speak helps open the door for deeper and more meaningful dialogue. Open-ended questions in particular pave the way for deeper understanding and insight – both for the person asking the question and for the person answering it. When asking open-ended questions, it is important to do so with genuine interest and a Care Frame online for a number of reasons. First, it helps others to feel psychologically safe. From neuroscience we know that feeling comfortable and safe helps keep the higher brain online and keep the threat response at bay. This is particularly important in communicating across differences. For some individuals, or in some particular situations, dialoging across differences can be perceived as threatening by the brain. The person asking the questions needs to be aware of this and intentionally engage a Care Frame by asking questions with sincerity, focused attention and an open mind in order to create psychological safety.

When we feel safe, the brain relaxes, and this provides an opportunity for someone to explore their own thinking and make new connections in their own thought processes. Neuroscience findings show that when people are encouraged to think through questions and problems on their own, it provides a stronger and more consistent pathway for gaining personal insight.[78] Moreover, experiments have found that analytical thinking is most effective for solving problems in which known strategies have been laid out for solutions (such as arithmetic), but in solving new problems without a set path for finding a solution, insight is often best. In other words, say the researchers, it's absolutely worth listening to your "aha!" moments.[79] Asking open-ended questions invites a person to think about things in their own way, and reflect on what the question means to them personally as well as the facts of a situation. Responding to sincere and caring open-ended questions helps take the brain out of habitual response patterns which is also a critical component of having integrated and insightful thinking and learning.[80]

Asking open-ended questions while engaging a Care Frame also provides benefits to the person asking the questions. Engaging appreciation towards others helps keep our own higher brain online and provides access to higher levels of self-awareness. We then have a greater ability to notice and manage our own thinking and the stories, assumptions and judgments that come up as we listen. This high level of awareness also allows us to consciously choose to listen through a lens of curiosity. Neuroscience research findings reveal a strong connection between curiosity and the brain's reward center. In a recent study, for example, researchers at the University of California, Davis conducted experiments with participants undergoing fMRI observation to discover what exactly goes on in the brain when our curiosity is aroused. One of the most significant findings was that curiosity helps make learning and working with others a more rewarding experience. The researchers found that when participants' curiosity had been sparked, there was increased activity "in the brain circuit that is related to reward and pleasure." [81] When we feel rewarded, this also positively influences our motivation to repeat the experience.

Consciously engaging curiosity also helps keep ourselves in an open, positive and receptive state. Activating a positive state in ourselves helps bring our own reward center online, and through our mirror neuron system influences the activation of the reward center in others, keeping them motivated to stay engaged in the dialogue, furthering an upward communication spiral. Engaging curiosity also helps us to listen more openly. As we've seen, the brain easily defaults to what it already knows, and when we encounter differences that are unfamiliar and/or cause feelings of discomfort it can destabilize our higher brain and diminish our ability – and motivation – to maintain genuine curiosity and interest in the person whose experiences are very different from our own. If the discomfort is strong enough, it might also trigger a threat response.

There are some general guidelines for asking open-ended questions that are helpful. These are presented below.

Open-ended questions often begin with the words "what," "how," or "why." For example:

What did you experience _____?
What are your thoughts about ____?
What do you think would happen if ____?
Why do you think they may have _____?
How do you see the situation?
How are you feeling about_____?
What are you learning from this?

When asking "why" questions it is helpful to be aware that even though "why" questions are open-ended, they can cause defensiveness unless they are asked with a nonjudgmental tone and open body language. Defensiveness can occur when "why" questions are asked in a manner that make people feel like they have to defend their actions or perspectives rather than explore their thoughts and feelings.

Engaging a Care Frame and asking open-ended questions is a way to regain a positive focus and direct our attention back to the other person. By engaging appreciation and positive regard for the other person, and bringing our own higher brains back online, we are better able to consciously override any discomfort and listen more openly and more deeply to what they are really saying. Staying in curiosity helps the brain hear and better understand someone else's unique experience or perspective, even if we have not experienced anything similar ourselves.

Step Three: Validate and don't interrupt

To validate someone's experience means that we listen with a specific intention to "hear" what they are actually saying. This is not easy for the brain. The Laboratory of Neuro Imaging states that the brain thinks between 50,000 and 70,000 thoughts per day, which means that we think between 35 and 48 thoughts per minute.[82] We need to be aware of this, because before a person has even finished speaking, our brains will have generated a multitude of thoughts, ideas, stories, beliefs – even conclusions – about what the person means. Listening to validate involves keeping high levels of awareness online so we can set aside our own agenda and listen beyond our own thoughts and experiences. In validating, we work to listen not just to the details and facts, but also to the perspectives, feelings, attitudes and beliefs that someone is conveying through their words and their body language. This takes practice, yet is not hard to learn. Sometimes referred to as metacognition, or having awareness of one's own thinking process, it involves the skill of "listening to our own listening," and noticing and setting aside our own internal thoughts and reactions.

Maintaining awareness of our inner wanderings, interpretations and judgments is essential to developing the ability to listen deeply, and it is also provides the opportunity to be aware of and override any biases, assumptions or judgments that show up. Being aware of our own internal processes gives us the opportunity to consciously choose to let go of our own line of thinking, re-engage positive regard, and refocus our attention on the speaker. This also provides us an opportunity to notice when we want to interrupt the speaker, and not to do so. Creating space for silence helps the speaker go deeper into their own thought processes.

When we validate others, they feel heard and understood, which allows the brain to move forward in a positive way. It also helps create resonance with each other. When there is resonance during the conversation, issues may not even be fully resolved, but there is a feeling of moving forward in a productive way. If there is not resonance, then people are more likely to lose brain energy and productivity re-hashing, reliving and rehearsing the conversation afterwards. When we validate others and really listen, people are much more willing to stay engaged and continue to work towards further understanding.

From an inclusion perspective, listening without interrupting is especially important because interruptions can devalue the person who is speaking, which can be very frustrating and feel like a microinequity. Furthermore, interrupting shifts the focus from the other person back to you, and sends an unintended message that what you have to say is more important. Research has shown how prevalent this pattern is in communications.[83] It's important to notice when we are interrupting and not listening to the other person, as this is very off-putting and damaging to the trust building process.

Listening without interrupting also creates pauses and moments of silence, and while this may cause some discomfort, these quiet moments are very important. They create space for curiosity, deeper reflection and the opportunity to have an "aha" moment. Research on insight shows that how much we are intentionally open and curious can affect whether or not we will have insightful thinking. Researchers at Drexel and Northwestern have also found that people in a positive mood were more likely to demonstrate both curiosity and experience insight.[84] Letting people speak without interruption and holding an intentional Care Frame helps set up both our brain and the other person's brain for insight and learning when we are communicating. Engaging a Care Frame is vital to learning to listen outside of what we know, and to staying open to what someone is actually saying. With a Care Frame online and listening without interrupting, our brains are less likely to fall into automatic responses that may seem innocuous to us, but may have the impact of completely discounting – or not "hearing" – what someone is actually saying.

Step Four: End with explicit positive regard

Step 4 brings the Care Frame and S.A.V.E. Communication Model together in a full circle. Ending the conversation with explicit positive regard means that we make an explicit and genuine statement of appreciation towards the other person, regardless of how the conversation went. If the conversation had difficult moments and was tense, or things did not get fully resolved, we still take the time to close the dialogue with appreciation. This last step communicates to the other person that you value and appreciate them as a person, and that you are willing to continue the conversation as needed to get the best outcome possible. The statement might be something as simple as "I appreciate your willingness to have this conversation with me. I know it may not have been easy, but I want you to know that I would like to continue talking and moving forward in new ways." Ending with positive regard communicates to the other person that you value them and care about their needs and perspectives. The statement of positive regard may also involve stating your respect for the differences between you, or even owning that you don't know what you don't know about their differences, and that you are willing to further educate yourself to learn more. When conversations end with a mutual feeling of positive regard, people are more likely to stay engaged and be willing to continue working towards a greater understanding of each other's differences.

It is also important to note that for those times when the conversation does not end well or with the outcome you want, it may feel counter-intuitive to the brain to end with a statement of explicit positive regard. And yet, we've seen how in engaging appreciation and keeping a Care Frame online, we have the best opportunity for operating from the higher brain, overriding discomfort, and making a conscious choice to act in a new way. From studies on neuroplasticity, we know that the act of actually practicing new behaviors – and especially those that take us out of pattern – creates new physical pathways in the brain, further advancing the brain's overall capacity to be more inclusive.

Summary

When we engage a Care Frame and practice the S.A.V.E. Communication Model steps on a regular basis, we actively support the brain going out of pattern and moving forward in ways that help connect us through our shared needs for psychological safety, validation, inclusion and the opportunity to bring our best selves to work. Engaging a Care Frame and practicing the S.A.V.E. Communication Model both stabilize the higher brain and help shape a more inclusive brain that supports inclusive behavior patterns and habits. Using this appreciation-based approach to communication in the workplace every day also has the beneficial effect of positively influencing the unconscious brain while helping to reduce psychological threats in the environment. All of this contributes directly to creating a more inclusive workplace.

So how can we put this all together in the moment? How do we notice when we are in a defensive reaction and the higher brain has gone offline? How can we incorporate strategies for working positively with the unconscious brain, manage and override the defensive brain, and engage an appreciation-based Care Frame, all while we are under the ongoing pressures, stress and urgency of the everyday workplace? What can help us manage our immediate reactions and defensive triggers, and also access higher levels of awareness in the moment?

A model and strategy called BrainStates Management™ provides the solution to these challenges. It is a powerful and easy to use in-the-moment tool that is based on recognizing and shifting brain states.

CHAPTER FOUR

Choosing Inclusion:
In the Moment Awareness

"Forever is composed of nows."
  - Emily Dickinson

Organizational research shows that today's work environments are increasingly filled with constant interruptions, shifting priorities, and increasing uncertainty. It is also clear that never before in human history have we been bombarded with as much information and with so many distractions as we now encounter on a daily basis. Moreover, many of these work environments are beginning to negatively affect people's ability to stay focused, direct their attention and maintain awareness throughout the day.[85]

Yet, despite these challenges, we always do have a choice in every moment. Each of us *can* learn to bring our attention to the present moment and become aware of our own reactions, and make choices about how we want to respond. A recent Harvard Business Review article underscores this point and emphasizes the importance of cultivating higher level awareness skills in order to monitor our internal reactions moment to moment, and to be able to respond consciously and in line with our values rather than just reacting to whatever is going on around us.[86] Awareness skills are the foundation for being able to make a conscious choice for inclusion in each moment.

The BrainStates Management™ Model offers a new framework for accessing higher levels of awareness in the moment by identifying and managing brain states. This model provides a practical strategy for accessing in the moment awareness and gaining direct insight into our current level of perception (open-mindedness), our capacity for System 2 thinking, and our ability to make conscious choices to override biases or discomfort, and act with behaviors of inclusion. The model is built on three interconnected aspects of the evolutionary brain, and provides the foundation for understanding and managing brain states.

The BrainStates Management™ Model Overview

Over the past several million years, our brains evolved into three distinct regions: the Reptilian Brain (lower brain) is the oldest region and, as we saw in chapter three, is tied directly to the threat response; the Limbic Brain (middle region) is involved in recording, storing and processing emotions; and the neocortex and prefrontal cortex, as we've seen, are the most recently developed areas of the brain. It is the seat of our higher cognitive functions and, as we saw in chapter one, is vital in our ability to be inclusive. These three brain regions correspond to following three brain states in the BrainStates Management™ Model, respectively: the Threat/Stress Response BrainState™, the Limbic Land BrainState™, and the Higher BrainState™. These are represented in the graphic below.

Three Brain Regions: Three BrainStates™

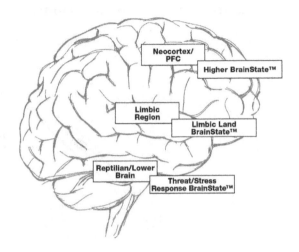

Next, the following three dimensions are added to the model: Perception, Conscious Choice and Self-Awareness. These three dimensions interact with the triune brain to form each of the three BrainStates™.

Perception: How open your brain's perceptual field is to new ideas and possibilities, seeing a bigger picture, and its ability to move forward towards achieving new goals.

Choice: The range and quality of the choices your brain has available, and whether your choices are being driven more by the unconscious brain or the conscious brain.

Self-Awareness: How much awareness and insight you have into your own thoughts and feelings, and your ability to understand what's driving your behavior.

BrainStates Management™ Model

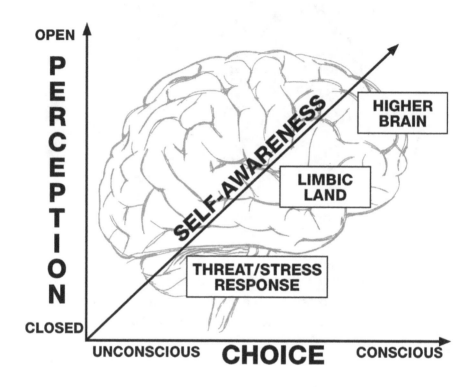

Looking at the model, the left axis represents perception and how open or narrow the brain's perceptual field is in each BrainState. Perception ranges from very open and being able to see a bigger picture and a wider range of options, to being closed and seeing very limited or no options. The bottom axis represents Choice and the range and quality of choices the brain has available in each BrainState. This dimension represents the degree to which one's choices, words and actions are being driven more by the unconscious brain or the conscious brain. Finally, the diagonal axis represents your level of Self-Awareness and how much insight you have into your own thoughts and feelings, and your ability to reflect on what is driving your behavior in each BrainState. This axis ranges from high self-awareness to very low self-awareness. As you can see, all three of these dimensions interact and directly influence the BrainState you are in.

Understanding BrainStates™

The following chart explains each brain state, and the available awareness within each one for acting out of pattern and consciously engaging in behaviors of inclusion across differences. Keep in mind that while each of the brain states is described independently, each brain region is highly complex, interdependent, and shares sophisticated interconnecting circuitry. Once we better understand each of the brain states at a high level, we can begin to look at strategies and tools to notice and manage them more effectively.

BrainStates™ Chart

Higher BrainState™	The Higher BrainState™ is where we have the highest capacity for self-awareness, and for making the conscious choice to go out of pattern and engage in positive actions across differences – even when it's uncomfortable to do so. From the Higher BrainState, we have the highest ability to hear and learn about the impact of our behavior on others, and the highest capacity for open-minded perceptions and the ability to see and generate new options and possibilities. In this brain state, we are most able to consciously engage a Care Frame™ and communicate across differences in open-minded and respectful ways. This brain state gives us our best opportunity to consciously practice the tools, strategies and skills needed to strengthen the social brain and build new neuropathways for demonstrating compassion, cooperation, and understanding across differences.
Limbic Land BrainState™	In the Limbic Land BrainState™ self-awareness is very unstable. This means there is a range of awareness in Limbic Land from pretty good awareness to low awareness, both of which directly affect our capacity for inclusion. In good awareness perception narrows and the availability of choices is reduced, but we still have the capacity to stay focused on tasks, get things done, execute routine decisions and be inclusive with those we are comfortable with. In low Limbic Land, we may intend to be inclusive, but in this lower range of awareness, perception is narrowed, and the availability of options and new choices is diminished, making it difficult to even have the motivation to access the higher brain. This also makes it more likely we will unconsciously act on unchecked assumptions, judgments and stereotypes and wind up confirming our biases rather than challenging them.
Threat/Stress Response BrainState™	In the Threat/Stress Response BrainState™ self-awareness is extremely low or it is completely off-line. This brain state involves the most closed perception and the tendency for the most unconscious choices, causing behavior to be driven by reactions and unconscious habits and patterns. It is characterized by "either/or" thinking and there is great difficulty in seeing options, or taking intentional and constructive actions. This brain state can be online for long periods, or it can occur as a quick reaction. In this brain state, there is an extremely low capacity for taking any out of pattern actions, engaging in inclusive and respectful behaviors, and being able to notice and manage one's biases and assumptions. This brain state is also characterized by a tendency to deflect and blame others or external circumstances for problems or issues.

As you read through the brain states in the chart above, it may have brought to mind times when you have experienced them in yourself, or have also seen them in others. We all experience going through different brain states throughout the day, and it is from our own personal experiences that we come to truly appreciate the difficulties that can come with Limbic Land or the Threat/Stress Response BrainStates™. Particularly, how operating from lower brain states can negatively impact relationships, team performance and organizational effectiveness. A conversation in a recent training session highlighted this when a participant came up to us to tell us something she was very excited about. She said that by learning about brain states, she was suddenly able to put a specific name on the negative dynamics that were affecting her entire team - lower BrainStates™! She shared that she could now see how her manager was inadvertently causing people's brains to go on the defensive. The manager adamantly wanted people to perform at higher levels, but by his behavior, he was actually putting people into Limbic Land or even the Threat/Stress Response – the very brain states that diminish the capacity for higher performance. She left the session also knowing how to notice and manage brain states in real time, and use it to help her team improve their performance.

BrainStates Management™: In the Moment Awareness

Learning to notice and manage brain states is what helps us access more awareness in the moment. It's important to recognize that BrainStates™ are dynamic and are constantly shifting. We've seen how today's workplaces are filled with pressure and uncertainty, and these kinds of conditions are particularly impactful on brain states. By learning to notice and manage brain states in the moment, we can better recognize when we are losing access to the higher brain, and make new choices. If the brain is not consciously managed in the moment, lower brain states can easily get triggered, impacting and reducing access to awareness, higher level thinking and the ability to consciously choose inclusive attitudes and behaviors.

Another aspect of brain states is they are directly impacted by our ever changing physical, mental and emotional states. On any given day, if we are feeling tired, or not feeling well, or have emotional issues going on, these states impact our ability to keep our awareness high and it is more difficult to keep the higher brain online. We have seen how the lower brain and the threat response impact awareness and perception, and we may find ourselves in the Limbic Land BrainState™ at any given moment – even though we are not consciously experiencing a noticeably strong threat response.

Limbic Land often involves underlying anxiety, worry or negative emotions being online. These underlying emotions can cause us to become caught in up in negative thinking/feeling loops and keeping us stuck in continually replaying a situation in our heads. We call this being "story absorbed." The more stuck we get, the more our emotions register in our body, making it feel even more "true," which fuels even more negative thoughts. Before we know it, we are so caught up in a story loop that it becomes almost impossible to see things differently, and we don't notice the impact it is having on our ability to operate from the higher brain. The story in our head can be so compelling that we lose the awareness that we are even out of awareness. Adding to this challenge, when someone's differences make us uncomfortable, their differences become a central plot line in our story generating the basic reasons why we feel the situation is difficult or unsatisfactory. In these moments, we need to be able to step back and recognize when our discomfort, biases and assumptions are being fueled by our narrowed perception and conditioned stories about others.

Learning to notice and manage brain states in the moment provides greater access to in the moment awareness and our ability to keep the higher brain online. While no one is in the higher brain 100% of the time, the good news is that we can develop brain skills to be there more consistently. An easy way to think about it is in terms of percentages and increasing the percentage of time we are in the higher brain during each day. Depending on what is going on, some days we may do better than others. To help us increase our percentages, what is needed is a practical approach for bringing the higher brain and increased self-awareness back online. BrainStates Management™ provides a platform for building our skills to notice and proactively manage our brain states.

BrainStates Management™ Skills

The purpose of BrainStates Management™ is to be able to access higher levels of awareness in the moment in order to operate from the higher brain more consistently. By understanding brain states, we can become more skillful at noticing our reactions and our level of awareness in each moment, and make more conscious choices to get back to the higher brain and be more inclusive in our thoughts, words and actions.

There are three key BrainStates Management™ skills that help us develop new, more positive inclusion habits and behaviors. They are:

- **Recognize** Your BrainState
- **Shift** to the Higher Brain
- **Maintain and Maximize** the Higher Brain

The first skill, "Recognize Your BrainState," involves learning to recognize our physical sensations, thoughts and emotions we are experiencing in any given moment. Once we have recognized what brain state we are in, the second skill is to re-engage the prefrontal cortex by using strategies and tools to "Shift to the Higher Brain." When we become adept at recognizing and shifting to the higher brain, the third skill comes into play which involves learning to "Maintain and Maximize the Higher Brain." This third skill helps us to operate from the higher brain more consistently by increasing the ratio of time spent in the higher brain vs. the lower brain states.

Consistently practicing these three skills is what helps build new neuropathways and establish new unconscious habits that support accessing and operating from the higher brain more consistently. Every time we use BrainState Management™ skills, we strengthen our ability to recognize and shift brain states which, like exercising a muscle, makes it easier to engage and maintain access to the higher brain and consistently choose attitudes and behaviors of inclusion in the moment.

Skill #1: Recognize Your BrainState™

The first skill of BrainStates Management™ is to recognize the brain state you are in, which is fundamental to gaining in the moment awareness. When we are in Limbic Land or the Threat/Stress Response our awareness may be so low - or even unavailable - that it is essential to have a quick, easy way to assess how much awareness is online (or not), and the degree to which we are operating from the higher brain (or not). As we've seen, self-awareness is a tricky business in the brain as it contains the central paradox that just when it's needed the most is when there is the least of it available.

We know that when the defensive brain gets triggered, it significantly impedes our ability to notice and override biases and assumptions, and consciously engage in behaviors of inclusion. However, by learning to recognize the current brain state we are in, we can gain in the moment information about our current level of perception, how much self-awareness is online, how likely we are able to override unconscious assumptions and biases, and choose attitudes and behaviors that demonstrate open-mindedness and respect. Recognizing brain states begins with first drawing our attention to our physical body and noticing our physical cues, and from there being able to identify the accompanying thinking and emotional cues in the moment.

The chart below shows some typical physical, thinking and feeling cues for each of the BrainStates. The chart begins with physical cues because learning to notice what is happening in our physiology is a key starting point for gaining awareness about what brain state we are in. The body doesn't lie, and it is constantly registering and reacting to what is happening whether we are consciously aware of it or not. We may tell ourselves that we're not upset, annoyed, frustrated, or worried, but somewhere these states are being registered in our physiology. If we learn to pay attention and recognize the specific cues our bodies, thoughts and feelings are sending us, we can gain significant information about the brain state we are in, and what we need to do next.

It is helpful to first read through the physical body cues for each BrainState, as these provide the initial red flags and early warning signals when we are going into a reactive state. Once you've read through the physical cues, then also read through the accompanying emotional and thinking cues associated with each BrainState. As you read through some of the typical cues – physical, emotional and thinking – be aware that they will vary from individual to individual and some cues may be more significant than others, and you may also have some that are not listed. You can add these, and can use this chart to reflect on and begin to notice your own personal cues of what shows up for you in your physiology, feelings and thinking in each brain state. This will be powerful information for you to be able to recognize your own brain state in the moment.

Recognizing BrainStates™ - Awareness Cues

Threat/Stress Response BrainState™	Limbic Land BrainState™	Higher BrainState™
Physical Body Cues: - Increased heart rate - Rapid breathing, higher up in chest - Sweating - Clenched teeth and jaw - Tightness in gut/ abdomen	**Physical Body Cues:** - Shift in breathing - Breathing is more shallow or higher in chest - Tense gut - Shift in heart rate - Tensed muscles	**Physical Body Cues:** - Relaxed muscles - Even breathing, lower diaphragm - Calm or energized - Normal heart rate - Relaxed jaw
Emotional Cues: - Strong negative emotions - Anger - Sad, despair - Fear, worry, anxiety	**Emotional Cues:** - Increased negativity - Uncertainty - Low level worry, anxiety or fear - Feeling stressed	**Emotional Cues:** - Happy - Contentment - Excited - Peaceful - Sense of wellbeing
Thinking Cues: - Negative - Blame external circumstance or people - See very limited range of options - Either/or thinking - Reactive	**Thinking Cues:** - Start to see limited possibilities - Can easily get caught in negative thinking/feeling loops ("awfulizing") - Less receptive to seeing another perspective - Reduced ability to focus on tasks	**Thinking Cues:** - Open minded - See possibilities, expansive - Positive - Proactive - Curious - Recognize multiple perspectives - Non-judgmental

By noticing and paying attention to our physiology and our personal physical cues, we can learn to recognize, in the moment, what brain state we are in. By first noticing our bodies' reactions, we gain awareness of how open or closed we feel; from this awareness we can raise the bar even higher and begin to notice our thinking and feelings. We can observe whether we are becoming more open-minded or not, and tune into any particular emotions that are online. To get good at identifying our thoughts and emotions takes practice, but it is a very important practice. It is in doing this that we start to gain information and insight into what is underlying our reactions - our assumptions, beliefs, judgments and expectations. Even just gaining awareness that we are losing awareness is really helpful information.

When we realize we are in a lower brain state and losing awareness, we can then know it is prudent to proceed with caution. For as we know, speaking and acting from a lower brain BrainState creates a high probability that whatever we say or do next will be unconscious, most likely defensive, and not very considerate of others or the bigger picture. Learning to recognize our own personal physical, emotional and thinking cues adds greatly in our ability to recognize when we are in a low brain state and gain enough awareness to avoid responding with strong negative reactions that potentially make things worse.

So what does the first skill – Recognize BrainStates – look like in real time? A recent client situation illustrates how using this first skill helped a team identify a negative communication pattern – in the moment – and change their approach using a Care Fame™.

In Real Time: Case Study

The department managers of a medical supply company were called to an urgent meeting by the company's CEO. In the meeting they were informed that quarterly earnings had come in lower than expected, and that the stock price was down. The managers were told to go back and send a strong message to their employees that this was unacceptable, and to make sure that every employee understood they needed to buckle down and work harder.

All of the department managers, including their boss Amanda, were upset by this mandate. For the past six months, their employees had all been working flat out to meet a number of very challenging deadlines. The managers felt that to now tell their employees they had to work even harder would cause animosity, make them feel unappreciated, and actually demotivate them.

Following the meeting, Amanda noticed the managers huddled together in the hallway all talking at once. As she approached them she noticed they were trying to keep their voices down (unsuccessfully), and exhibiting a lot of negative body language. Seeing this, Amanda's first thought was, "Here we go again." As she watched them, the negative communication patterns she so often saw in other challenging situations were definitely happening again.

Amanda understood why they were upset – she didn't agree with the mandate either – but she had real concerns about how the team was managing their reactions and how able they would be to move forward in a positive direction. Whenever upper management decisions were mandated, it caused the team to spend considerable time and energy rehashing all the reasons why they didn't agree, which reinforced even more frustration, sending them into a downward spiral of negativity. This was an old pattern, and something the team had discussed a number of times, but it had never resulted in them doing anything differently. While the team's current reactions were frustrating for Amanda, she was also well aware that this situation provided the exact opportunity they needed to take a risk and try something new. She called a meeting for later that afternoon.

The Meeting

At the start of the meeting, there was still a lot of negativity and tension in the room. Amanda was aware that peoples' lower brains were completely triggered. She noticed that people were not listening to each other and were acting with considerable defensiveness and unconscious negative behaviors. She noticed some individuals becoming even more adamant that they were right as the threat response took over and their perceptions narrowed. She took a deep breath and persevered.

Amanda began by acknowledging the difficulty of their situations with their employees. She then went on to remind them of the BrainStates Management training they had taken two weeks earlier, and suggested this would be good opportunity to practice the new skills. Howard, who was still very upset, was the first to speak. He said, "Are you kidding me? Those brain state things? Those are skills for easy discussions. This is a real situation that has to be changed." Linda agreed and said, "This is completely unacceptable. Top management has absolutely no regard or respect for the amount of work our employees have already been doing, not to mention the stress they've been under, and then to add on to it? Where are these senior leaders' heads? They are completely out of touch with our employees." Another manager chimed in, "We have to tell senior management that we are not going to put our employees under any more stress."

At that point Amanda intervened and asked the group to stop talking. Without much explanation, she handed out a worksheet to each person and said, "Complete Part I of this worksheet, and then we'll continue the conversation." A little taken aback about why they were doing this in the middle of a very important discussion, they individually began their work. Part I of the worksheet had one question to answer. It read: "*What do you notice in your body right now?*" It provided some suggestions of things to notice and consider, such as their breathing patterns, heart rate, areas of muscle tightness, tension or strong physical sensation. A few minutes later, when each person had completed their worksheet, the energy in the room was noticeably calmer.

Amanda opened the conversation by asking them to share what they had written. Slowly at first, the managers began to share how paying attention to their physiology was giving them new awareness about their physical state. Linda shared that she was now aware of having a strong clenched jaw. Rajeev shared that his breathing had been fast and his shoulders were tense. Another person shared they were aware of having a tight gut. Someone remembered a line from the training – "that the body doesn't lie" – and everyone laughed. They described how coming into physical body awareness had brought them into "in the moment" awareness and they could see that they were in a strong reaction state.

As a result of identifying their physiological cues, more team members expressed an increasing level of awareness of themselves in the moment. A few also mentioned that once they recognized their physical cues, they were also aware of the accompanying thoughts and feelings. Martha shared that in noticing she had a tight gut, she suddenly became aware that she was thinking about how much she disliked conflict, and her feelings were of wanting to check out and avoid it. Amanda asked her what her dislike of conflict was about, and after reflecting for a moment Martha realized it was an old pattern from the past. She was also now aware that she could intentionally focus on changing her behavior in these situations. Luis said he noticed he had gone into very reactive thinking and was blaming top management and accusing them of being completely out of touch with reality. He laughed as he shared this, noting how he made a sweeping generalization that is not true; there have been plenty of times he has agreed with the direction and decisions of the top leaders.

Other team members were also discussing their increased awareness and insights into their reactions. Amanda saw the opportunity to then direct them to the second part of the worksheet. It was a two-part question that read, "*Reflect on and note any of the thoughts and feelings you are aware of experiencing, and identify the BrainState™ you were operating from.*" In discussing this question, there was a lot of new energy in the room as people began connecting their reactions – their physiology and accompanying thoughts and feelings – with their BrainState. People reported being in either Limbic Land or the Threat/Stress Response BrainState; no one reported being in the Higher BrainState. The group talked about this and the impact it has on their ability to communicate effectively and to make decisions as a team.

The team discussed how they could use the skill of Recognizing Your BrainState in handling issues and reactions going forward. Amanda then asked the group to discuss the last question on the worksheet which read, "How can you apply your new awareness and insights to the situation with the Senior Leaders from earlier today?" It was slow at first, but as the conversation got underway, people starting suggesting different ideas and options that would have been rejected out of hand at the beginning of the meeting. One suggestion in particular caught the group's attention. What if they asked for a meeting with the senior leaders to discuss what *they as managers could do* to be more effective in working and communicating with the Senior Leaders. People realized this approach was very different from their normal way of dealing with the senior leaders, but many team members were intrigued. They discussed how this kind of approach might engage the Senior Leaders in a non-defensive way. This approach also might start a new kind of conversation, one that didn't begin with judgments and negative assumptions. A team member then offered another potential benefit: how this kind of approach could help both the managers and the senior leaders manage any potential threat responses, which would allow for more effective communication and problem solving from the higher brain.

As the discussion progressed, Amanda was aware that there were still a couple of team members who seemed disengaged, particularly Howard. Howard hadn't written anything down to the questions, and he seemed to be getting increasingly frustrated as the conversation went on. She turned to him and asked how he was doing. Immediately, and in a very strong and frustrated voice, Howard said, "I don't get any of this. The decision those executives made was straight up wrong, and they've been doing it for far too long. Why am I supposed to try and look at this more openly? What about what they need to do? They're the problem here."

To Amanda's surprise, Howard's comment started an interesting conversation among the team. The managers who were considering there may be a better, less stressful way to look at and approach the situation, started trying to influence Howard to look at his own reactions first, *before deciding* on how he wanted to approach the senior leaders. Individuals suggested that Howard take stock of his current physiology, and use the worksheet to recognize his physiology, thoughts and feelings to identify the BrainState he was operating from. But Howard wasn't influenced at all, and had no interest in the rest of the group's growing interest in moving forward differently. Howard remained steadfast in his belief that the Senior Leaders needed to be held accountable for how they continually disrespected and ignored the managers' needs and important perspectives, especially regarding the situation earlier in the day. That was the only conversation Howard felt was worth having. In that moment, Howard was in a Threat Stress Response BrainState, and his perception was so narrow that he was not able to access any awareness of his own limited view. Howard would need additional tools and skills to recognize his current brain state and be able to access higher levels of awareness.

In this real time example, we can see that it is common for people to move through different levels of awareness at different times or, in some instances, not at all. In some situations we can open our perceptional view more easily and consider other options. Yet, at other times, it can be extremely challenging. This can be especially true when it is something that challenges our strongly held beliefs, such as Howard's belief that senior managers shouldn't act the way they did. Our stereotypes, assumptions and beliefs about people's differences can also make it challenging to see things differently, or even realize we are carrying a story about them that isn't actually connected to who they really are.

As we've seen, sometimes a recognition of our current state is all we need and we can simply shift, as some of the team members were able to do. Other times, it may be more challenging to shift brain states and re-engage the higher brain. Just like Howard, we can all get stuck and unable to see things differently. That's when we need additional tools and strategies to intentionally shift brain states and reengage higher levels of awareness, perception and conscious choices in order to make a positive change in our behavior.

Skill #2: Shifting to the Higher Brain

The work place is filled with potentially upsetting situations that can easily trigger a threat response and bring the dynamics of the defensive brain online. We know that when peoples' lower brains are triggered, there is less access to open-minded perceptions, and there is an increased likelihood that people will act out of unconscious behavior patterns and stereotypes. Given this, it is easy to see how individuals in challenging situations can continue in a downward spiral of misunderstandings, negative assumptions and accusations. But what if that didn't happen?

What if challenging situations could be handled differently in the moment? What if all the individuals involved could gain enough awareness to manage their own brains in the moment and make new, more conscious and inclusive choices? What new outcomes might be possible if we had the tools and skills to recognize our lowered levels of perception, awareness and choices, and we were able to shift to the higher brain in the middle of the tension and discomfort? This may seem like a tall order, but it is very possible to learn to do, and the brain is actually very capable of supporting us in this process.

Neuroscience is shedding some interesting new light on the brain's innate ability to shift perception and see the world differently. In one experiment, for example, participants were given prism inversion glasses to wear which inverted everything they saw around them. As they looked through the inversion glasses, all of their perceptions were turned on end so that the room and everything in it was turned upside down. Then, as the participants went about conducting ordinary tasks such as walking or reading, the perceptual centers in the brain quickly flipped so that everything in the room appeared right side up. When they removed the glasses, once again things appeared upside down, then the brain adjusted and everything went back to appearing right side up again.[87] Just like that.

From this and other studies we can see that when it comes to shifting perception, the brain is fully capable of doing so. It isn't the brain that makes it challenging to shift perception and see things differently. Rather, it's our own ability and willingness (or unwillingness) to consciously use tools and strategies that bring higher levels of awareness and perceptions back online. The *brain* is fully capable of seeing through a lens of inclusion, compassion and cooperation, but whether this capacity is engaged is a choice that is entirely up to us. Indeed, the choice to be in the moment, and to see the world through an inclusive lens, is what will build new neuropathways of awareness. From neuroscience we are also learning that even though awareness is an internal state, it is comprised of neural connections, and these neural awareness connections can be trained and strengthened in the brain through practice.[88] Just like working out in the gym, we have to build new awareness muscles. When we practice engaging higher level perceptions, it also lends itself to discovering higher level outcomes, and this is rewarding and motivating to the brain. We need to make it a practice, for unless we try it a few times and see the benefits, we won't ever be motivated by these new outcomes to try it again. So how do we do it?

The tools for Shifting to the Higher Brain are described below. These tools provide easy, practical and straightforward ways we can gain a small amount of awareness to intentionally move ourselves towards more awareness – even when we feel stuck – and even perhaps when we have tried to previously shift without success. There are two categories of shifting strategies and tools presented: tools that can be used in the moment, and those that can be used at a later time - especially when getting a new perspective is proving to be difficult. As you consider the list of shift tools below, you might think of other things you do that also work for you to help you shift brain states. Having a variety of shifting tools and strategies is extremely beneficial so you have different ones you can employ depending on the situation. If one tool is not helping you to make a shift, you can try another. The shift tools are presented below in these two categories of "in the moment" and "tools for later."

Shifting BrainStates - In the Moment Tool

Pause and breathe intentionally. Take slow deep intentional inhales and exhales, and continue to do so until you notice a calming of the physiological responses in your body. Slow, steady, intentional breaths help bring the nervous system into balance, and calm the body's physiology.

This helps the body and brain relax, and can restore a small window of awareness we can use to stop the downward cycle of the defensive brain reactions.

If you find it difficult to calm your physiology and get it to a more neutral state, there are a couple of options:

- Continue the slow deep breathing and use any of the additional in the moment tools until you find your body calms to a neutral state.
- Acknowledge you are having a strong reaction and need more time to shift. This is especially helpful if your physiology continues to be strong and your ability get any awareness online remains diminished.

Consciously engage appreciation-based tools. Using the tools and strategies from Positive Priming, Engaging a Care Frame and the S.A.V.E. Communication Model will help you to access your higher brain, and they will also influence others' brains in positive ways. Cultivating feelings of appreciation directly supports our ability to re-engage the higher brain, as positive feeling states stabilize the prefrontal cortex.[89] Laughter can also help us access more positive feeling states and help us shift in the moment. Laughter is like a car wash for the brain.

Engage short term memory by focusing on a task. Short term memory in the brain is associated with the prefrontal cortex. It can have the effect of getting enough awareness online that the body calms down and the ability to focus returns. This may not always take you to a full Higher BrainState™, but it can facilitate enough cortical activity to keep functioning at a more neutral level, which helps keep you productive and prevents you from losing more energy. Counting to 24 by 3's, for example, engages short term memory and helps bring the higher brain back online. Focusing on a specific task, and listing the specific steps you need to take is one way to bring short term memory back online.

Ask yourself questions that can help facilitate a shift:

- How could I see this differently? This is a good question to bring open-mindedness, options and creativity back online. The brain loves novelty, unsolved puzzles and options, and asking yourself this question can engage these, all of which are tied to the higher brain.

- <u>What outcome do I want?</u> This is also a good in the moment question and shifting tool because in order to become aware of outcomes, the brain has to think about the future, which engages the higher brain. This is helpful in shifting to higher self-awareness as it also helps interrupt System 1 thinking and unconscious, habitual patterns and responses.

Shifting to the Higher Brain - Tools for Later

Look for any underlying beliefs, expectations or needs that may be contributing to difficulty in shifting out of a lower brain state. Typical ones are:

- The need to be right / fear of being wrong
- The need to look good in front of others / fear of making mistakes, not being perfect
- The need to feel competent / fear of not feeling competent
- Beliefs and expectations about how the world "should" work
- Beliefs and expectations about how people "should" act

Move and Do. If you find yourself stuck and unable to make a shift, do any of the following with the conscious intention of shifting and seeing things differently:

- Talk it out with a friend
- Go for a walk in nature
- Do physical exercise
- Read something with an uplifting message
- Meditation, yoga or other centering practices
- Reach out to others who are in a positive feeling state
- Do something good for someone else
- Other helpful, favorite things that put you in a positive state

Look for a Silver Lining. Work on developing the viewpoint that things don't happen to us, they happen for us. How we frame our world directly influences our unconscious expectations, and this approach allows us to see challenging or undesirable events and situations in ways that give us insight and information for how we can be more in line with our personal values and intentions. Even in the midst of bad events, good can come from it. Ask yourself, what is good about this situation? What is now possible that wasn't possible before this undesirable event or interaction occurred?

It is possible to think, act or feel our way into shifting to a higher brain state. Try any of the tools and strategies presented here or others you prefer until you feel a shift. Once there is even a small opening in our awareness, we can work towards re-engaging the higher brain and our ability to see the bigger picture, consider different options and possibilities, and be open to more creative and effective outcomes. As you practice the shift tools and strategies, pay attention to any particular ones that work most effectively for you and help you personally shift into a better state. One colleague shared that her child is very adept at noticing her moods, and if she seems stressed or upset, her daughter will give her a hug and tell her to "just breathe and let it go," helping her to focus her attention and make a shift.

It is also important to note that sometimes shifting takes time and additional work. There may be times we can't make a shift and the best we can do is to acknowledge it and be gentle with ourselves. We can remind ourselves that there are other choices, options and more positive ways of responding, we just can't see them yet. If we can see these situations as opportunities to learn about ourselves - our unconscious expectations, beliefs, assumptions and patterns, we can come back to it later and explore what may be preventing us from making a shift, such as a limiting belief, assumptions we may be making, or being caught up in a negative thinking/feeling loop. Learning to shift to the Higher Brain helps us align with our highest and best selves in the moment, and be better able to respond to ourselves and others with kindness and understanding.

Learning to recognize and shift brain states not only benefits us individually, it also can benefit an entire team. As we saw in the example with Amanda and her managers, recognizing BrainStates and using shift tools helped their team break out of an unproductive communication pattern that they had struggled with. As the team members worked to recognize and shift their individual BrianStates they were then able to help others shift and move the conversation to a much more productive level and create better outcomes.

Another team we worked with said they noticed immediate improvements in how their diverse team functioned after learning BrainStates Management and practicing the skills. They talked about how they are much more aware of the impact they have on each other and are more intentional in how they communicate with each other. They now pay closer attention to how people react and respond, and if they notice each other going into Limbic Land or the Threat/Stress Response BrainStates™, they call it out and talk about it. The more we work to recognize and shift BrainStates™, the more readily we can then use the third BrainStates Management™ skill: to Maintain and Maximize the Higher Brain.

Skill #3: Maintain and Maximize the Higher Brain

The third skill in BrainStates Management is to "Maintain and Maximize the Higher Brain." This skill involves strengthening our ability to keep the higher brain online more consistently. As mentioned, no one is in the higher brain 100% of the time, yet we can consciously increase our percentages. A key aspect to maintaining access to the higher brain involves noticing when we are there. Building this recognition of when we are in the higher brain is equally as important as building recognition of Limbic Land and the Threat/Stress Response BrainStates.

We can learn to recognize how our body feels and the quality or nature of our thoughts and feelings when the higher brain is online. It feels good to be in a positive, open and receptive state. Think about how you feel when you are at your best, and notice the specific qualities and characteristics of when you are your best self. What does your body feel like? How would you describe your thinking and your feelings? By identifying these qualities, you can strengthen your capacity to be in the higher brain more of the time, even when under stress or in challenging situations.

Keeping the higher brain online is supported by positive feeling states. As we saw in chapter three, when the positive brain is online we can access higher levels of personal insight, as well as increased creativity. Engaging positive feeling states not only stabilizes the higher brain, it also facilitates higher levels of perception and the ability to see an even broader range of choices. From an inclusion perspective, maintaining and maximizing the higher brain is where we can intentionally repattern our biases and responses to differences. We can be most successful in building new be-havioral habits that are inclusive, and consciously override the "us vs. them" defensive instincts of the brain. We can use the appreciation based tools to build deeper, more meaningful connections and trust-based re-lationships across differences. Using the S.A.V.E. Communiation Model helps maintain access to the higher brain and primes the pump for curi-osity and listening outside of what we already know.

From what we know about neuroplasticity, the more we are in the higher brain and consciously extend empathy, care and compassion across dif-ferences, the more we strengthen the brain's ability to do this on its own. We set the neurological conditions for our future now, in each moment. Placing our attention on maintaining and maximizing the higher brain not only will improve our performance and productivity as we work across differences, we will shape a more inclusive brain in the process.

Summary

Using the skills of recognizing and shifting brain states consistently, and especially practicing them in the moment, will help the brain gain familiar-ity and comfort with the process, and this will strengthen the associated neuropathways. The goal of BrainStates Management is not to do it per-fectly every time, because that isn't realistic. Overall, the goal is to increase the brain's ability to more frequently and consistently shift to the higher brain, and maintain and maximize access to it. This process is also greatly supported by understanding and developing seven key dimensions of neuroscience that help us to both shift brain states and maintain and maximize the higher brain. Building competency in these seven dimensions is also vital in shaping a more inclusive brain and creating a bigger we.

CHAPTER FIVE

Building a Larger Circle of We

"Our task must be to free ourselves by widening our circle of compassion to embrace all living creatures and the whole of nature and its beauty."
– Albert Einstein

We are at an unparalleled juncture in the evolution of the human brain. Standing at this evolutionary intersection of conscious choice, each of us either participates in increasing the brain's capacity for inclusion, or not. Each of us chooses to either consciously evolve our brains towards a greater capacity for open-mindedness, compassion, respectfulness and cooperation, or we unconsciously reinforce the brain's "us vs. them" dynamics and preferences for ease and comfort, and forgo the opportunity to build a more inclusive brain.

Choosing to consciously build the brain's capacity for inclusion means we can increase the brain's overall capacity to readily extend care, cooperation and compassion across differences, while supporting the brain in being able to create a bigger circle of we. There continues to be compelling new research into the brain's ability to increase these social brain capacities. For example, Dr. Tania Singer at the Max Planck Institute for Human Cognitive and Brain Sciences in Germany, has conducted seminal research on empathy and compassion. Her research shows that individuals can increase their capacity for compassion through specific training, and this activates brain networks associated with affiliation with others, and the reward circuitry in the brain.[90] Science is now making it clear that we choose the brains of our future by the attitudes and behaviors we consciously and unconsciously engage in today. Making a conscious choice to show compassion, care and kindness towards others whose differences are unfamiliar or uncomfortable today is how we strengthen the social circuitry across differences, and consciously participate in shaping a brain that is more inclusive and fundamentally more capable of extending a larger circle of we.

We've seen how the skills of recognizing and shifting brain states help establish new neuropathways that strengthen our ability to access and operate from the higher brain, as well as override the dynamics and tendencies of the defensive brain. These skills are critical in demonstrating respectful behaviors across differences more consistently, and they directly support us in building new inclusion habits. Yet, to truly increase the brain's overall capacity for inclusion, and ensure the ongoing opportunity to build a larger circle of we, requires understanding the third skill in more detail: the skill of Maintaining and Maximizing the Higher Brain.

Maintaining and Maximizing the Higher Brain

The skill of maintaining and maximizing the higher brain involves understanding that advancing the brain's overall capacity for inclusion is a percentages game. Over time, as we create new inclusion habits, the brain becomes more accustomed to operating from higher levels of awareness and seeing more options and possibilities. As this happens, our desire to operate from higher level perceptions and make choices that result in new options and outcomes starts to become an integrated part of who we are. By continuing to practice these new behavioral habits we actively participate in shaping a more inclusive brain. For example, studies show that intentionally practicing internally created states of kindness and compassion can become an enduring trait of the individual, as reflected in long-term changes in brain function and structure.[91]

There is a famous quote, often attributed to Gandhi, which says: *"Our thoughts become our words, our words become our actions, our actions become our habits, our habits become our character and our character becomes our destiny."* These words are very wise indeed, and in light of what we now know about neuroplasticity and our ability to consciously evolve our brains, they are also very prescient. What we think, how we feel, what we say, and the actions we take every day shape our brains and our entire physiology towards care, cooperation and compassion across differences or not, depending on our choices. Advancing the brain's capacity for inclusion means making the choice for higher levels of awareness and perception until it becomes integrated into the fabric of who we are. We can become more and more adept at recognizing when lower brain perceptions come online, and see them for what they are – brain survival circuitry – and not the truth of who we or others are, or who we are choosing to become. This is how each of us individually participates in overriding and re-patterning the brain's "us vs. them" orientation, and contributes to building a bigger circle and creating a larger we.

We need to build the brain's overall capacity for inclusion by expanding and sustaining even greater levels of self-awareness, compassion and appreciation within ourselves first. To become truly capable of extending the circle of we beyond our current levels of comfort and familiarity, we need to shape a brain that goes beyond its current architecture to ensure the dexterity necessary for the 21st century. To do this, there are seven neuroscience-based dimensions that underlie our capacity to build a more inclusive brain, and we can intentionally strengthen and leverage these dimensions in order to extend the circle of we even further. The seven dimensions are as follows:

- Metacognition
- Physical Body Awareness
- Brain Energy
- Attention/Positivity
- Actions/Behaviors
- Underlying Beliefs
- Shifting BrainStates

The descriptions of the dimensions below highlight *how* each dimension uniquely contributes to maintaining and maximizing the higher brain, and increasing our overall capacity to shape a more inclusive brain. It is important to note that given the complexity and interconnectivity of the brain, these seven dimensions are not independent of each other, and developing any one of the dimensions has the effect of positively strengthening the other dimensions as well. As such, the dimensions are not presented in any particular order.

Seven Dimensions

Metacognition

This dimension directly supports shaping an inclusive brain by helping us become more aware of how our meta thoughts - that is, the thoughts behind our thoughts, and how they influence our perceptions, choices, decisions and behaviors throughout the day. The competency of metacognition involves bringing into conscious awareness the constant undercurrent of thoughts that go on behind (meta) our conscious thoughts all day long. It involves the ability to "think about one's thinking," and helps us notice and reflect on the thoughts behind our thoughts (sometimes referred to as "mental noise") and become more aware of how this constant stream of mostly background thoughts directly influences our attitudes, perceptions, moods and behaviors throughout the day – whether we are consciously aware of them or not.

For example, the simple act of going to the supermarket might be accompanied by conscious or unconscious thoughts such as: *Why didn't I do this yesterday when I was right by there? Groceries are getting so expensive, and I haven't had a raise in two years.* Or, *These apples look delicious, and so do the pears, I guess I got here at the right time. I'm excited to get home with all this wonderful food for my family.* This ongoing stream of meta-thoughts is where our biases, judgments and negative assumptions of others easily hide out. We can't manage what we can't see, and by developing and strengthening metacognition, we get better at noticing how our "under the radar" biases operate, what stories they tell us, and how they influence our behaviors – positively and negatively – when they go unnoticed.

In addition to strengthening our ability to notice and challenge our thoughts and assumptions, the competency of metacognition also helps us to gain awareness of the associating feelings, as it is a two way street. Our thoughts influence our emotions, and vice versa. Both of these impact our ability to challenge and override our assumptions or biases, and our ability to choose the thoughts and feelings that lead to building connections and trust with others outside of our comfort zone. Increasing this inner awareness opens the space to make new choices in our perceptions and behavior, and increases our ability to be inclusive. For example, we know that communicating across cultures is often very challenging and can easily result in miscommunication or misinterpreting each other's messages. Research is showing that strengthening metacognition is tremendously beneficial in communicating across cultures more effectively. Studies have found that having strong metacognition skills *coupled with* cultural knowledge have improved cross-cultural communication, and result in higher levels of collaboration and trust.[92] These same studies show that only having knowledge of cultural practices *without also* having metacognitive awareness can lead to more stereotyping, lower collaboration and trust.

Mindfulness and the Brain

Research shows that we can strengthen our metacognition skills and abilities through mindfulness training. Mindfulness training is a specific practice for strengthening awareness of one's thought processes and related feeling states, and is often defined as the practice of maintaining a nonjudgmental state of heightened or complete awareness of one's thoughts, emotions, or experiences on a moment-to-moment basis.[93] Recent neuroscience studies on mindfulness training show that it helps cultivate a receptive mental state while it also enhances growth in the middle prefrontal regions of the brain, where key aspects of the brain's social circuitry reside.[94] Strengthening our capacity for metacognition and mindful awareness has also been shown to help individuals override and decrease bias. For example, studies by Adam Lueke and Bryan Gibson at Central Michigan University show that mindfulness training can help decrease implicit out-group bias, as measured on the Implicit Association Test.[95]

Physical Body Awareness

We've seen how noticing our physiology and physical cues helps us to recognize our brain state in the moment. Increasing our competency in this dimension further increases our ability to notice and use the body's physical and emotional signals more consistently. Developing more intentional awareness of our body's ongoing physical sensations and states helps us be more in tune with our own emotions and reactions, and increases our ability to be more emotionally intelligent with others. This dimension also reflects how much intentional care we put into our physical body. Science is making it ever more clear that adequate sleep, exercise and nutrition are essential to the brain and the body's optimal functioning and have a direct impact on both the availability and the quality of our brain energy every day.

Research from many health and science disciplines show that our emotions are stored in the body, and are tied to physiological changes such as alterations in blood pressure, heart rate, and body temperature. The ability to tune into these physical changes and sensations is a direct link to becoming more aware of our emotions. For example, psychologist Dr. Eugene Gendlin developed a therapeutic technique called "Focusing" that helps people name and connect up with their emotions by having them first identify areas of physical sensation in the body. Starting with developing an awareness of physical sensations, and then noticing the associating thoughts and feelings afterwards, is a reversed process that has proved to very effective with many people.[96] Increasing awareness of our physical body and subtle changes in our physiology provides us a direct path for insight into our thoughts and emotions.

Our emotions and the associated physical sensations and signals can be very subtle, making them easy to miss and go on unnoticed. Research is showing that there are structures in the brain toward the middle of the prefrontal cortex that provide vital connections between our thoughts, emotions and the physical body.[97] This connection can be accessed by learning to pay more attention to our bodies' physical sensations and signals. Rather than ignoring or overriding the information our body is giving us, we can use the information to gain insight and heighten self-awareness.

Tuning in to our physical body more consciously throughout the day is a tangible way to gain more awareness of our underlying thoughts and feelings, and helps us uncover any negative assumptions, biases and judgments we may have about others' differences, and be able to make more conscious choices about them. The dimension of Physical Body Awareness gives us additional information and insight that we can use to keep moving forward in building more authentic connections across differences, which aids us significantly in shaping a more inclusive brain. Additionally, reading the body's signals is a helpful tool when we decide to take a risk, go out of pattern, and engage in new behaviors.

Going out of Pattern

When we decide to move towards connecting with others who are different from us in ways that are unfamiliar or cause us discomfort, it is not a straightforward process in the brain. Dr. Greene and others talk about how consciously extending compassion and understanding towards those we perceive to be outside of our "tribe" goes against the brain's base instincts, and this can feel very counter-intuitive to the brain. Our long established neuropathways, patterns and maps shape our views of the world – and our brains – creating a powerful sense of what is "normal" for each person. When these established pathways and unconscious world views are challenged by engaging in new attitudes and behaviors, it can cause extreme discomfort in the brain and we also feel it in our physical bodies. Consider this simple example.

Let's say you buy a car, and the tires are out of alignment which causes the car to pull to the right. You drive the car for several weeks, and eventually, you stop noticing that it pulls to the right because the lack of alignment starts to feel normal. Later, when you take it in and have the alignment corrected, there is a good chance that when you drive away, the perfect alignment will not feel "right." Even though you know logically that having your tires in alignment is important for both your car and your safety, it can still feel like it's not "normal." When we know something is logically correct, but it doesn't yet feel right or normal, it can cause an uncomfortable transitional state referred to as "cognitive dissonance," and this discomfort also registers in our bodies.

In building a more inclusive brain, it is important to know that the experience of dissonance can happen and that the best way to manage it is to keep practicing the new behaviors – even though it may feel uncomfortable at first. The more we practice new behaviors (i.e. drive the car with the corrected alignment), the more we establish new corresponding neuropathways in the brain. The more established these neuropathways become, the less dissonance we feel. Eventually, these new behaviors become unconscious habits, and become an integrated part of who we are and what we feel is normal.

It's important to develop the ability to notice and tolerate dissonance, otherwise we will be drawn back to the comfort of our old behaviors - even though we know these behaviors are not in line with who we want to become. Acknowledging that the behavior change process can feel counter-intuitive helps us tolerate any dissonance that may occur as we act in new ways to connect and build relationships with others who our brains may not regard as members of our "in group." Over time, this process gets more familiar, and our ability to tolerate dissonance in the behavior change process improves, until eventually we create a new normal. By increasing our awareness of our body's signals, we can recognize and understand that it is uncomfortable as the brain works to establish new physical pathways that support our new behaviors. Tolerating dissonance is a critical component of building a more inclusive brain.

Brain Energy

It takes extra brain energy to engage System 2 thinking and operate from the higher brain throughout the day. This dimension indicates how well we consciously manage our brain energy in order to keep sufficient awareness available for challenging our assumptions and biases and being able to consciously engage in new, more inclusive thoughts and behaviors.

Neuroscience findings reveal that the brain energy we have available every day is both limited and easily expended. As we saw in chapter two, the brain is an energy hog, using over 20 percent of the body's total energy every day. We need to make choices about how we spend it, or it can become significantly depleted before the day is finished. For example, we need brain energy to go out of pattern and engage in new behaviors, manage dissonance, challenge our assumptions and biases and carry through on our new decisions and choices. All of this takes brain energy *in addition* to what we need for our regular daily tasks. In building a more inclusive brain, it is important to be very intentional in how we both use and conserve our brain energy, otherwise, we won't have sufficient brain energy to establish new behavior patterns and build a more inclusive brain.

There are a number of common things that easily drain brain energy throughout the day. For example, constant distractions and interruptions while trying to concentrate. We like to think we can conserve brain energy by multi-tasking, but the research is telling us that it actually does the opposite. Multi-tasking on two or more cognitive tasks is really continuous "task switching" which requires the brain to switch focus and attention back and forth from one task to another. This is shown to reduce task efficiency and accuracy while also using more brain energy.[98] We think multi-tasking increases our overall efficiency, yet we are actually using valuable brain energy that we need available to keep the higher brain, self-awareness and System 2 thinking online. Other common brain energy drains include getting stuck in negative thought/ feeling loops, and worrying and ruminating about things we can't control (other people, organizational dynamics, workload, traffic, the weather, etc.). Research also shows that making decisions that involve emotions, uncertainty, and unclear choices uses significantly more brain energy than routine decisions.[99]

There are innumerable ways that each of us uniquely burns unnecessary brain energy every day. Yet, there is good news. Each of us *can* learn to manage our brain energy more effectively by becoming more aware of how we spend or conserve it throughout the day. For example, noticing and shifting brain states is an effective strategy as it brings awareness back online so we can consciously choose specific behaviors that both conserve our own brain energy, and also have a positive effect on the environment. Research shows there are some additional strategies that are important for maintaining or boosting brain energy during the day. Overall, the most effective way to conserve and boost brain energy is develop competency in any (or all) of the other six dimensions.

Boosting Brain Energy: Sleep, Diet and Exercise

Research shows that we can exercise, eat a healthy snack, take a 20 minute nap, or meditate if we need to give our brain energy a boost during the day. However, the only solution for fully restoring the brain's energy tank is to get a good night's sleep. There is also mounting evidence that insufficient sleep negatively impacts brain functioning by decreasing our cognitive functioning, including short and long term memory. Sleep deprivation is also shown to: reduce the brain's ability to take in information, undermine analytical effectiveness and good decision making, and decrease the brain's ability to process emotions effectively.[100] Some research shows that even just getting 2-3 less hours of sleep than you need can slow reaction time by 50% compared to someone who is well rested. (Notably, a 50% reduction in reaction time has the same impact on cognitive performance as when someone can be considered legally drunk.) In getting sufficient sleep to adequately restore brain energy, seven to eight hours is generally recommended, although it varies individually.

Diet and exercise also impact the brain's overall functioning and availability of energy throughout the day. Eating healthy foods that are low on the glycemic index (which shows how slowly or quickly foods cause increases in blood glucose levels) supports optimal brain and body functioning, and is one of the things that can restore some amount of brain energy during the day. Regular exercise is shown to boost brain energy as well, and is also shown to improve memory and thinking. Studies have found that regular aerobic exercise increases the size of the hippocampus, a critical region associated with memory and learning. Studies have also shown that the prefrontal cortex and medial temporal cortex, areas that control thinking and memory, have a greater volume in people who exercise compared to people who don't. Dr. Scott McGinnis, a neurologist at Brigham and Women's Hospital and an instructor in neurology at Harvard Medical School, states that recent findings show that non-exercisers who start a program of regular aerobic exercise of moderate intensity for 6-12 months show an increase in the volume of these brain regions.[101]

Attention/Positivity

This dimension is related to the appreciation-based strategies and skills discussed in Chapter 3, and goes further in strengthening our overall capacity for sustaining positive feeling states to increase our effectiveness across differences. It includes focusing on what is happening in the moment, and intentionally looking for what is good. We know from the research that appreciation and positive feeling states benefit our physical and mental capacities, and help the brain stay open-minded and aware by strengthening the social brain. Positive emotions are also correlated with staying connected to our purpose and core values, and keeping an open heart toward others' needs, beliefs, values and perspectives. In terms of building a more inclusive brain, there are additional benefits that cultivating and sustaining positive feeling states provide. This practice helps us direct our attention towards what is positive in other people and situations, and supports our ability to show compassion, kindness and care towards ourselves and others.

The Institute of HeartMath® has done extensive research on the impact of positive feeling states on the brain, heart, body and mind. HeartMath's key discoveries are based on their research into the impact of emotions on the electrical pattern of the heart. When we experience negative emotions, this creates disordered or chaotic electrical patterns in the heart. When we experience positive emotions, this creates ordered and coherent electrical patterns. These electrical signals of the heart are 40-50 times greater in amplitude than any other electrical patterns in the body, and they are communicated to every cell in the body. Their research shows that learning to generate positive feeling states in oneself, and sustain them for as little as five minutes, brings the electrical signal of the heart into a state of "coherence." This state is experienced as a state of calm, heightened awareness and insight. Notably, this state of coherence is also correlated with higher cortical functioning.[102]

Compassion

Compassion helps strengthen the social circuitry of the brain, making it easier to extend care and kindness towards others we may not consider to be like ourselves. Studies on compassion show that it is a softer state and is different from empathy. When we show empathy towards someone who is experiencing negative emotions, it can actually increase negative emotions in ourselves. Additionally, as mentioned earlier, empathy does not engage as readily when our brain perceives someone as an "other" and unlike ourselves. Compassion, on the other hand, uses different circuitry in the brain, and unlike empathy with its tendency to not engage when we see someone else as not part of our "tribe," engaging compassion actually promotes feelings of affiliation with others.[103] Dr. Srini Pillay refers to this ability as developing "cognitive compassion."[104]

We've seen that the ability to extend compassion to others can be strengthened, and that kindness and compassion-based meditation practices can further strengthen the capacities of the social brain. These studies also show that we don't have to practice compassion-based meditation practices for very long to improve the brain's ability to be more open-minded and kind towards others. Dr. Richard Davidson, Professor and Director of the Waisman Laboratory for Brain Imaging and Behavior at the University of Wisconsin-Madison, has conducted studies that compare what happens in the brains of Tibetan Buddhist Monks as they practice compassion-based meditation with what happens in the brains of novice meditators using the same compassion-based meditation practices. Using fMRI technology and scanning the brains of both groups as they actively meditated, the findings showed that the monks' *and* the novice meditators' brain scans both had increased activity in brain regions that monitor emotions, plan movements (action center), and generate positive feeling states like happiness.[105]

Dr. Davidson also found that the monks' brains had stronger connections between the prefrontal cortex and the emotional regions in the brain, enabling higher thinking and an ability to notice and manage emotions. In his review of these findings, Dr. Davidson emphasizes that while the monks showed more capacity given their extensive mediation experience, it is also clearly established that compassion-based meditation practices can be learned quickly, as evidenced by the students. From the monks' brain scans we see that ongoing consistent practice leads to a greater capacity for compassion, but the initial benefits are also available with little training or upfront investment. Furthermore, other studies on a compassion-based meditation called "loving-kindness" meditation show that these techniques can actually reduce bias towards others.

In one particular study, researchers looked at how loving-kindness meditation might reduce prejudice. To set a baseline prejudice score, researchers used the Implicit Association Test (IAT). The IAT test measures individuals' reaction times as they match up positive and negative words, for example, happiness or wrong, with faces that belong to either their own or another ethnic group. This produces a "bias score." Generally, people are quicker to match positive stimuli with their own group and quicker to match negative stimuli to the other group. The IAT test is considered by many to be a more accurate reading of someone's implicit or unconscious biases.

In conducting their study, the researchers enrolled a sample of 71 white, non-meditating adults and gave them the Implicit Association Test to determine their initial baseline prejudice score. Each participant was then given a photo of a black person who matched the same gender as themselves. Following this, participants were then given either (a) a tape with loving-kindness mediation instructions on it, or (b) a set of instructions on how to look closely at the photo they were given and notice certain features of the face. Both conditions lasted just seven minutes. At the end of that period, every participant took another IAT test.

Their new results showed that in just seven minutes, those that participated in the loving-kindness meditation directed towards a member of a specific racial group (in this case, a black person) was sufficient to reduce racial bias towards that group. However, there was no measurable reduction in racial bias by the group that focused on the photograph of a black person without accompanying meditation.

In addition to bias reduction, the researchers also measured different kinds of positive emotions the meditating group experienced. The research showed that their positive emotions were more "other-regarding" (e.g. love, gratitude, awe, elevation) as opposed to self-orientated (e.g. contentment, pride). These other-regarding emotions also correlated more strongly with scores that showed a reduction in bias.[106] Additional studies on compassion-based meditation practices also show that the brain areas that track and differentiate what is self and what is other become quieter – essentially helping us become more open-hearted towards others. This suggests that the more we practice compassionate-based meditation techniques, the more we can directly influence the structure of the brain, and shape a brain that helps us override our base instincts and demonstrate attitudes and behaviors of inclusion across differences with more consistency and success. Developing a greater capacity for compassion allows us to move forward in our ability to override and re-pattern biases, assumptions and the "us vs. them" tendencies of the brain, and helps shape a brain that is better able to collaborate, build trust, and work together more cooperatively and effectively.

Where We Focus Our Attention

Where we choose to focus our attention every day matters. Living in an age where we are bombarded with external stimuli constantly vying for our attention, it can be very difficult to consistently focus attention on the things that are most important. For example, a recent study asked executives to respond to this specific question: "I spend much of my time reacting to immediate demands rather than focusing on activities with longer-term leverage." Eighty percent of the executives agreed with this statement.[107] It's no wonder why neuroscientists, such as Dr. David Strayer, refer to effectively directing attention as "the holy grail" of success.

Where attention goes, neural firing occurs, and where neurons fire, new connections are made. What we pay attention to — in little and big ways — is what determines whether we consciously participate in building a more inclusive brain or not. Yet, with practice, we can learn to direct our attention, and one very helpful way is to look for and focus on what is positive. Our attention is a resource we can use to increase awareness of what *is* working, what we are doing that is already great, and keep gratitude and appreciation online. We can use our attentional resources to keep the brain tipped toward framing the world in positive ways by noticing what is positive in ourselves, in others, and in situations through-out the day. This helps us to see possibilities instead of limitations, hold curiosity instead of judgment, and be willing to listen to another point of view or different opinion. Directing our attention to what is positive supports shaping a brain that is more inclined to perceive differences as opportunities for connection and collaboration rather than to see them as a threat.

Directing our attention to what is positive also supports our ability to stay focused on the outcomes we are trying to create. Focusing on outcomes means thinking about the future, and, as mentioned, the brain can only think about the future when the prefrontal cortex is engaged.[108] This means that focusing on outcomes automatically brings the higher brain online. Focusing on outcomes also helps bring our attention to the things that are most important, and provides a "check in" on whether the work processes and dynamics we're engaged in are effective or ineffective in achieving the outcomes we're after. This information and insight can then be used to recalibrate our attention towards the outcomes we are after, and conserve brain energy in the process.

We also need to consciously turn the dial down on distractions in order to conserve energy and direct our attention more judiciously. Research by Dr. Strayer shows that deliberately stepping away from all of our electronic devices, for even just a few moments at a time, benefits our attentional resources and also positively affects memory and learning. Dr. Strayer states that "Everything that you're conscious of, everything you let in, everything you remember and you forget, depends on it (the ability to focus our attention)." He advocates that we intentionally take breaks and step away from our devices to rest the brain and increase our ability to focus our attention.[109]

Actions/Behaviors

This dimension reflects how aware we are of our behaviors (verbal and non-verbal) and how they impact others. Our tone of voice and non-verbal gestures send messages to others that we are often not even aware of. Through the brain's mirror neuron system, and other aspects of the social brain, our non-verbal behavior such as arm gestures, facial expressions, tone of voice and physical stance are all replicated in another person's brain. Their brains pick up and mimic our non-verbals, which directly influences how they hear our message even though the process goes on unconsciously.

This dimension also involves our ability to stay open and listen non-defensively to hear and learn how our specific behaviors are impacting others, and what we can do to be more respectful and inclusive. It is important to be open to feedback from others, especially across differences because many of our non-verbal signals are unconscious and we are often not aware of their impact on others. For example, someone's differences may trigger an unconscious bias that causes us to tense up, fold our arms, use less eye contact, and send other "closed" messages with our body language. These unconscious non-verbal behaviors can send a message of "less than" and may be experienced as a microinequity by some individuals. While it is not possible to remain fully aware of all the ways that our attitudes and behaviors affect others throughout the day, we can learn to stay open to feedback from others and increase our awareness of what behaviors we need to change. Even if the feedback we receive doesn't make sense to us based on our own life experiences, we still need to keep listening. This is how we gain new awareness about the messages we are sending unconsciously through our body language that are having a negative impact on others. Using the S.A.V.E. Communication Model can be a helpful tool when having these conversations as it supports non-defensive and appreciation-based conversations. Being open to hearing how our behaviors impact others is also a powerful way to learn about others' different needs and perspectives, and what we need to do specifically to demonstrate inclusion behaviors more effectively.

Another very impactful way to help ensure that our non-verbal messages are positive is to Engage a Care Frame. Engaging a Care Frame puts *us* in a positive state of appreciation, and this registers in every cell of our body directly affecting the subtle messages we send. Our facial expressions, how our bodies move, our stance, tone of voice, eye contact and the myriad of other unconscious signals that we send are shown to be more positive when we are in a positive emotional state ourselves. In this way, our non-verbal behaviors are more likely to unconsciously send a message to others that we care, that they matter, and we see them as important and valued. When we hold people in explicit positive regard and use appreciation-based skills, we send coherent signals and create shared understanding with others.

Studies also show that demonstrating positive intent and positive emotions improves our ability to more accurately recognize both facial expressions and gestures in others.[110] Noticing other people's non-verbal behaviors gives us cues about the message they are sending. This information also provides another excellent opportunity to use the S.A.V.E. Communication™ model to listen outside of what we already know. This can help us gain a deeper understanding of someone's message and what they may *not be* saying, as well as learn more about who they really are. In strengthening this dimension, we directly influence the conscious and unconscious verbal and non-verbal behavior messages we send to be more positive and inclusive, and through the mirror neuron system, this helps establish an upward communication spiral, and supports creating a more emotionally positive work climate overall.

Underlying Beliefs

This is perhaps the most challenging dimension in building our capacity for a more inclusive brain. Our deepest beliefs about the world make up what is normal for us, and as we've seen, when we challenge what feels normal it can be a very uncomfortable experience. Our beliefs can be so embedded in the brain that to challenge them – even when there are clear reasons to do so – can create such dissonance that we simply disregard the challenging information. Consider the following study that highlights the difficulty of changing underlying beliefs in the face of countering, factual evidence.

In the study, a group of adults each took a standard eye test and received their results. This same group then took a second eye test, only this time the chart was reversed with the smallest letters at the top of the chart and largest letters at the bottom. After receiving their results from the second eye test, something interesting happened. It turned out that more than 60% of the group showed improved eyesight on the second exam.

Researchers speculated that this was related to the participants underlying beliefs and unconscious expectations. The first exam with the bigger letters at the top may have triggered an unconscious expectation that the smaller letters would be harder to read as they moved down the chart. In the second exam when the small letters were at the top, the participants didn't have an unconscious expectation that the smaller letters would be harder to read. As a result they were able to read more of them and get a more accurate reading of their eyesight. What happened next was particularly interesting, and underscores how underlying beliefs can make the behavior change process more difficult.

More than half of the people with improved eyesight on the second exam refused to believe it was a more accurate result, and insisted that the first exam more accurately reflected their eyesight – even in the face of the counteracting data. Even though the second exam showed them they could actually read more letters, these results were dismissed out of hand.[111] This study demonstrates how dissonance and discomfort, when they are not recognized and managed, can significantly interfere with our ability to see the world in new ways.

This study also sheds light on how our unconscious beliefs translate into our expectations, and how these expectations get confirmed in our experiences. Our brains prefer what we already know because there is no discomfort or dissonance involved. This is why we need to manage dissonance when challenging our beliefs, or we will simply become more entrenched in our assumptions and stereotypes and continue to demonstrate the same biases and negative behaviors towards others. Memory also plays a role in reinforcing our underlying beliefs as it strongly influences how we experience the present based on what we have experienced in the past. Research shows that all of our experiences are captured in the unconscious and become part of our implicit memory, shaping implicit mental models and beliefs.[112] Strengthening our ability to examine underlying beliefs aids us in challenging the inherent biases and assumptions that come with our conditioned mental models.

When we *do* step outside of our old ideas and conditioned behavior patterns and try something new, we need to recognize and manage any accompanying dissonance or we will be tempted to fall back to the comfort of what we already know, and continually miss opportunities to see things differently, and get a better, higher level outcome (i.e. read the small letters more accurately). Learning to tolerate and manage dissonance is what takes us beyond our current habits and makes it possible to engage across difference more positively and effectively. Recognizing and overriding dissonance gives us the opportunity to go out of pattern, and truly open to new possibilities, deeper insights and greater understanding in building connections across differences, thereby also supporting the process of shaping a more inclusive brain.

When someone's differences threaten our beliefs – consciously or unconsciously – we can use our physical body signals and cues as well as our metacognition skills to manage the dissonance involved. We can use these competencies to honestly evaluate how our existing beliefs impact our ability to demonstrate inclusive and respectful behaviors – or not. Once we have determined that certain underlying beliefs, assumptions or values no longer serve our ability to be inclusive, this is the beginning of creating real change in ourselves, and in creating new possibilities and new outcomes in our relationships with others. It is also helpful to remember that when we have a strong reaction to something, it's an opportunity to check for any underlying beliefs that might be driving our reaction. We can get in the habit of honestly evaluating whether our underlying beliefs lead us closer to our goal of more inclusion, or whether they get in our way. Questioning and challenging underlying beliefs is an inclusion competency that leads to letting go of old ways of thinking and creating new, more positive experiences across differences, while building the capacity to hold space for new possibilities and new outcomes to emerge. These are key new habits in our journey of building a more inclusive brain.

Shifting BrainStates

This dimension indicates our ability to consistently recognize what brain state we are in, and use tools and strategies to bring the higher brain back online. Increasing our overall capacity to shift brain states involves cultivating the willingness to let go of lower level perceptions sooner and with less resistance, and at the same time be willing to operate from the higher brain, and allow new possibilities and out of pattern events to emerge. This is not always easy for the brain, and it takes time to build this competency. Yet the more we consciously shift brain states and access higher levels of awareness and perceptions, the more familiar and comfortable the process becomes. Over time, we can learn to shift brain states even during challenging or stressful situations, or during (or shortly after) a strong emotional reaction. Building our capacity to shift brain states also helps us become more adept at noticing and setting aside negative thoughts and feelings until we are ready to deal with them, and supports directing our attention to the present moment while also conserving brain energy.

In shifting brain states more consistently, we build a strong experiential knowledge base that lets us trust that there are always new choices available in every moment, even if they are not readily apparent. Shifting brain states also supports cognitive flexibility which is a key skill in working across differences and in working across cultures, in particular. Shifting brain states improves our capacity for tolerating any dissonance and discomfort that arises when encountering unfamiliar cultural norms, and the cultural assumptions about what is "normal" that get triggered. With a greater competency in shifting brain states we can engage the higher brain and access more awareness of our own thoughts and feelings, which provides greater mental flexibility and ability to effectively communicate across the sometimes very large gap of different cultural assumptions, and what each person considers to be "normal."

Shifting brain states more consistently develops an ongoing awareness that we create the world we see based on what brain state is dominating in any given moment. Strengthening this dimension helps us recognize more quickly how our reactions are driven by the internal brain dynamics of perception, awareness and choice, and the impact these have on our expectations, needs, fears, and actions. With this understanding, we get better at recognizing and letting go of lower brain state perceptions, and become willing to open to other perspectives and consider things outside of our own experiences. As we increase our brain's dexterity in being able to shift more easily in the moment, we also become more adept at preventing ourselves from going down the proverbial rabbit hole in the first place. We become more skilled at recognizing old patterns or underlying beliefs that lead us nowhere new, and we also get more willing to go through whatever dissonance shows up because we recognize the value in doing so is paramount to our own learning and development, and in developing more inclusion skills and shaping a more inclusive brain.

A New Way Forward: A Path for Peace

In strengthening the seven dimensions, we build a more inclusive brain – one that is capable of extending kindness, care and compassion across differences. According to neuroscientist and Nobel Prize winner Gerald Edelman, the brain is capable of making one million billion synaptic connections. He states that if we considered all the possible neural connections the brain is capable of making "we would be dealing with hyper astronomical numbers: 10 followed by at least a million zeros."[113] There's an infinite number of ways the brain can make connections, and yet how specific connections and circuitry are laid down is unique in each individual. We can consciously create new synaptic connections through the experiences, thoughts and emotions we choose in how we respond to and interact with those who are different from ourselves.

We are in new times. Diversity is growing at an unparalleled rate in organizations, and this carries with it an increasing possibility for unconscious biases and stereotypes to create conflicts, misunderstandings and "us vs. them" dynamics. Yet, just as the potential for these dynamics increases, brain science also offers this new way forward. Studies show that we can decrease prejudice and develop meaningful relationships across groups by reducing anxiety, feelings of threat and uncertainty.[114] Our brain-based models, tools and strategies provide ways to reduce fear, override dissonance and counter-intuitive feelings and make a new choice to move forward in ways that allow for honest dialogue, understanding, collaboration, and greater trust across differences. We now have the information, strategies and tools to consciously recognize and consciously override and re-pattern the base instincts of our brain, and manage dissonance effectively as we create something new. In building and strengthening the pathways for care, compassion and kindness in our own brains, we create a positive influence on others' brains at the same time, and in the process make inclusion and respect an integrated part of an organization's culture.

We've seen that our brains are exceptionally capable of developing a greater capacity for inclusion, as well as strengthening existing circuitry for extending care to others outside of our comfort zone. Yet the desire to keep an open mind and an open heart doesn't occur just because we think it should, or because we hope it will. It occurs because we try it, and discover that we like what happens when we let higher level perceptions guide our actions. It is still a percentages game, yet we begin to calculate the math differently. Over time, our experience convinces us that the more we operate from a place of willingness to see and act with an open mind and compassion towards ourselves and others, the easier it becomes to trust that new options and possibilities will become available and be entirely in our best interest.

Engaging a Care Frame and approaching conflict situations using the S.A.V.E. Communication Model, we find out that we can move beyond our unconscious assumptions and keep the brain moving forward. We might also begin to discover that winning an argument or believing our perspective is the only "truth" becomes less interesting than continuing to listen and finding out something we didn't know before. Or we may find ourselves using appreciation tools that positively prime the work environment because it feels good to *us* to do it. As we use the skills in BrainStates Management to recognize and shift brain states, we experience more and more of the benefits of re-engaging and keeping the higher brain online, paving the way for new, more inclusive thoughts and behaviors.

Our brains will continue to recycle the biased thoughts and feelings that arise from our past conditioning, but we get much better at discerning between these and the thoughts that occur naturally when we shift to the higher brain. Over time, our brains get accustomed to not being in conflict, we become quicker to forgive ourselves and others, and we start to prefer a higher state of being where we aren't absorbed in resentments from the past or have unmanaged anxiety about the future. In this a state of internal coherence, we authentically create external resonance with others and unconsciously shift the interpersonal dynamics in ways that are positive and help establish a bigger circle of we.

It is now a simple fact of science that we can make the choice to build a more inclusive brain. Speaking at the American University in 2016, the Dalai Lama said it this way: "We face a lot of problems, many of them our own making, arising as they do from anger and self-centeredness. But we can change. We can use our brains to learn to extend our concern to others...if we take a calm and compassionate approach I believe we can create a better, more peaceful world."[115]

BrainStates Management™ Self-Assessment

Note: If you are interested in getting feedback about your capacity in each dimension and additional skill building tips, you can take the BrainStates Management™ Self-Assessment at:

http://assessment.brainskillsatwork.com/assessment

Endnotes

INTRODUCTION.

1   Committee Encouraging Corporate Philanthropy. (2010). Shaping the future: Solving social problems through business strategy. *Pathways to Sustainable Value Creation in 2020*. Retrieved from http://cecp.co/wp-content/uploads/2016/11/Shaping-the-Future-1.pdf?redirect=no.

CHAPTER ONE. Why Good Intentions Are Not Enough

2   Association for Psychological Science. (2014, September 8). Faces are more likely to seem alive when we want to feel connected. *ScienceDaily*. Retrieved from http://www.sciencedaily.com/releases/2014/09/140908135421.htm.

3   Wellesley College. (2015, August 4). Prejudice causes the perception of threat: Study suggests that threat can be used to justify actions that result from prejudice. *ScienceDaily*. Retrieved from http: www.sciencedaily.com/releases/2015/08/150804074251.htm>.

4   Greene, J. (2013). *Moral Tribes: Emotion, Reason and the Gap Between Us and Them*, New York, New York: Penguin Books

5   Pillay, S. (2014, March 13.) How to Deal with Unfamiliar Situations. *Harvard Business Review*. Retrieved from https://hbr.org/2014/03/how-to-deal-with-unfamiliar-situations.

6   Gutsell, J., Inzlicht, M., (2010). Empathy constrained: Prejudice predicts reduced mental simulation of actions during observation of outgroups. *ScienceDirect*. Retrieved from https://www.brandeis.edu/departments/psych/gutsell/docs/Gutsell-Inzlicht-2010.pdf

7   American Psychological Association. (2011, September 1). Perception of facial expressions differ across cultures. *ScienceDaily*. Retrieved from http://www.sciencedaily.com/ releases/2011/09/110901105510.htm.

8   Wolfe, P. (2016, August 17.) Is a top college worth it? Is the cost of a top college worth it? It depends. Retrieved from http://blog.indeed.com/2016/08/17/is-a-top-college-worth-it?

9   Brooks, C. (2016, May 8.) Is your subconscious affecting your hiring decisions? Business News Daily. Retrieved from http://www.businessnewsdaily.com/5847-avoid-hiring-bias.html#sthash.I5qITrYt.dpuf

10   Jeffrey, R. (2014, June 22.) Inside the neuroscience of bias. Retrieved from https://www.wict.org/programs/conference/Documents/PeopleMgtBiasArticle.pdf

11   Fiske, S., Harris, L. (2006, October 17.) Dehumanizing the lowest of the low neuroimaging responses to extreme out-groups, *NCBI*. Retrieved from https://www.ncbi.nlm.nih.gov/pubmed/17100784

12   Fiske, S. *Ibid*.

13   Duke University. (2016, April 30.) Task force on bias and hate issues. *Task Force on Hate and-Bias Report*. Retrieved from https://spotlight.duke.edu/taskforce/wp-content/uploads/sites/2/2016/05/Final-Report-from-Task-Force-on-Hate-and-Bias-Issues.pdf

14 Swarns, R. (2015, October 30.) Biased lending evolves, and blacks face trouble getting mortgages, *New York Times*. Retrieved from https://www.nytimes.com/2015/10/31/nyregion/hudson-city-bank-settlement.html?_r=0

15 Roets, A. (2011, December 30.) Prejudice is a basic human need. *Science 2.0*. Retrieved from http://www.science20.com/news_articles/prejudice_basic_human_need-85802

16 Scientific American Mind. (2008). Buried prejudice. The bigot in your brain." Retrieved from https://www.scientificamerican.com/article/buried-prejudice-the-bigot-in-your-brain/

17 Mlodinow, L. (2012). *Subliminal: How Your Unconscious Mind Rules Your Behavior,"* New York, New York, Pantheon Books

18 Lieberman, M. (2013) *Social: Why Our Brains Are Wired to Connect,* Oxford, United Kingdom: Oxford University Press

19 Stiles, Joan, Jernigan, Terry L. (2010, December 20.) The basics of brain development. *SpringerLink*. Retrieved from https://www.ncbi.nlm.nih.gov/pmc/articles/PMC2989000/pdf/11065_2010_Article_9148.pdf

20 D'Or Institute for Research and Education (IDOR). (2001, December 15). Functional networks in emotional moral and non-moral social judgments. Retrieved from http://ltc-ead.nutes.ufrj.br/constructore/objetos/functional_networks_in_emotional_moral_and_nonmoral_social_judgment.pdf

21 Doidge, N. (2007). *The Brain That Changes Itself: Stories of Personal Triumph from the Frontiers of Brain Science,* New York, New York, Penguin.

22 Doman, Glenn. (2002). *What To Do about Your Brain Injured Child.* Garden City, New York: Square One Publishers.

23 Davidson, D. (as cited in Graham, L. 2013, p. xxviii) "what we focus on is what we get."

24 Amodio, David (2010, August 31.), The egalitarian brain, *Greater Good Science Center,* Retrieved from http://greatergood.berkeley. edu/article/item/the_egalitarian_brain|

CHAPTER 2. The Unconscious Brain and the Power of Appreciation

25 Ellen J. Langer (2009) *Counterclockwise: Mindful Health and the Power of Possibility,* New York, New York: Ballantine Books

26 Morgan, N. (2014) *Power Cues: The Subtle Science of Leading Groups, Persuading Others, and Maximizing Your Personal Impact,* Brighton, Massachusetts: Harvard Business Review Press

27 Gladwell, M. (2007) *Blink: The Power of Thinking Without Thinking,* New York, New York: Back Bay Books

28 http://www.iwpr.org/initiatives/pay-equity-and-discrimination Institute for Women's Policy Research, The Gender Wage Gap, 2014

29 University of Chicago Graduate School of Business. (2003, Spring Vol. 4 No. 4). Racial Bias in Hiring: Are Emily and Brendan More Employable than Lakisha and Jamal?, *Capital Ideas: Research Highlights.* Retrieved from http://www.chicagobooth.edu/capideas/ spring03/racialbias.html.

30 U.S. Bureau of Justice Statistics, (2014, September 30) https://www. bjs.gov/content/pub/pdf/p13.pdf

31 Harvard Business Review. (2014). Investors prefer entrepreneurial ventures pitched by attractive men. *PNAS Scientific Journal.* Retrieved from http://www.hbs.edu/faculty/Publication%20Files/Brooks%20 Huang%20Kearney%20Murray_ 59b551a9-8218-4b84-be15- eaff58009767.pdf.

32 University of Washington (2014, May 19). Favoritism, not hostility, causes most discrimination. Citation: ScienceDaily. Retrieved from http://www.sciencedaily.com/releases/2014/05/140519160609.htm.

33 Eagleman, D., MD, (2011). *Incognito: The Secret Lives of the Brain*. New York, New York: Vintage.

34 Azar Beth Azar. Your Brain on Culture November 2010) Your Brain on Culture, *APA Monitor on Psychology*. Retrieved from http://www.apa.org/monitor/2010/11/neuroscience.aspx

35 Bargh, J., (2012, January 18). Behavioral Priming: It's All in the Mind, but Whose Mind? *Plos One*. Retrieved from http://journals.plos.org/plosone/article?id=10.1371/journal.pone.0029081

36 Bargh, J. (2014, January). How unconscious thought and perception affect our every waking moment: Unconscious impulses and desires impel what we think and do in ways Freud never dreamed of. *Scientific American*, pp. 23-37. Retrieved from http:// www.scientificamerican.com/article/how-unconscious-thought-and-perception-affect- our-every-waking-moment/.

37 Kahneman, D. (2011). *Thinking, Fast and Slow*. New York, New York: Macmillan.

38 University of Pittsburg School of Health Sciences. (2016, January 4). Racial bias may be conveyed by doctors' body language. *ScienceDaily*. Retrieved from https://www.sciencedaily.com/releases/2016/01/160104130816.htm

39 Profiles in Diversity Journal (2004, January/February). The DNA of Culture Change. Retrieved from http://insighteducationsystems.com/PDF/DiversityJournal2004.pdf.

40 Vozz, S. (2015, January 5). The Discouraging Link Between Depression And Women In Power. *Fast Company Magazine*.

Retrieved from https://www.fastcompany.com/3040484/
strong-female-lead/the-discouraging-link-between-
depression-and-women-in-power

41 Morsella, E. (2015, June 26). Why you're pretty much unconscious all
    the time. *Time Magazine*. Retrieved From http://time.com/3937351/
    consciousness-unconsciousness-brain/

42 University of Pennsylvania School of Medicine News Release (2006,
    July 26). Penn researchers calculate how much the eye tells the
    brain. *Eureka Alert!* Retrieved from https://www.eurekalert.org/
    pub_releases/2006-07/uops-prc072606.php.

43 Perspectives on Psychological Science (2010). Culture Wires
    the Brain: A Cognitive Neuroscience Perspective. *Sage Journals*.
    Retrieved from http://doi.org/10.1177/1745691610374591.

44 National Academies Press (US). (2013, January 13). In the Light of
    Evolution: Volume VI: Brain and Behavior. The Remarkable, Yet Not
    Extraordinary, Human Brain as a Scaled-Up Primate Brain and Its
    Associated Cost. Retrieved from *NCBI*. https://www.ncbi.nlm.nih.
    gov/books/NBK207181/.

45 Doidge, N., MD (2007). *The Brain That Changes Itself: Stories of
    Personal Triumph from the Frontiers of Brain Science.* New York, New
    York: Penguin Books.

46 National Geographic Society. (2012). *Your Brain, A Users Guide: 100
    Things You Never Knew.* Washington, D.C.: National Geographic
    Society, publisher.

47 Kahneman, D. *Ibid.*

48 Thibeault, A.D. (2014). *An Executive Summary of 'Thinking, Fast and
    Slow' by Daniel Kahneman.* New York, New York: CreateSpace
    Independent Publishing Platform.

49   Kahneman, D. *Ibid.*

50   Child Development. (2009, Volume 80 (4)). Empathy is associated
      with dynamic change in prefrontal brain electrical activity during
      positive emotion in children. *NCBI Resources.* Retrieved from https://
      www.ncbi.nlm.nih.gov/pmc/articles/PMC2717040/.

51   Fredrickson, B. L. (2012). Leading with Positive emotions. *Center for
      Positive Organizations.* Retrieved from http://www.bus.umich.edu/
      FacultyResearch/Research/TryingTimes/ PositiveEmotions.htm.

52   Child Development. *Ibid.*

53   British Psychological Society. (2012, October 26). How the negative
      trumps the positive in politics. *ScienceDaily.* Retrieved from http://
      www.sciencedaily.com/releases/ 2012/10/121026084643.htm.

54   Fredrickson, B. L. (2012). Leading with Positive emotions. *Center for
      Positive Organizations.* Retrieved from http://www.bus.umich.edu/
      FacultyResearch/Research/TryingTimes/ PositiveEmotions.htm.

55   Fredrickson, B. L. (2009). Positivity: Groundbreaking Research
      Reveals how to Embrace the Hidden Strength of Positive Emotions,
      Overcome Negativity, and Thrive. New York: Crown

56   Fredrickson, B. L. (2009). Positivity: Groundbreaking Research
      Reveals how to Embrace the Hidden Strength of Positive Emotions,
      Overcome Negativity, and Thrive. New York: Crown

57   McCraty, Rollin. (2007). The relationship between heart-brain dy-
      namics, positive emotions, coherence, optimal health and cognitive
      function. *Coherence In Health.* Retrieved from: http://www.coheren-
      ceinhealth.nl

58   Instituto D'Or de Pesquisa e Ensino. (2014, May 21). Training
      Brain Patterns of Empathy Using Functional Brain Imaging.
      ScienceDaily. Retrieved from https://www.sciencedaily.com/releas-
      es/2014/05/140521180016.htm.

59 Human Resource Management Review. Performance management and employee engagement. *ScienceDirect*. Retrieved from http://www.sciencedirect.com/science/article/pii/S1053482210000409.

60 Schlossberg, M. (2016, February 27). Google experiment reveals the single most important quality for teamwork. *Business Insider*. Retrieved from http://www.businessinsider.com/google-reveals-how-to-have-the-perfect-team-2016-2.

61 Color Magazine. (2010, April). Micro-Affirmations: The Antidote to Workplace Inequities. *Issuu*. Retrieved from https://issuu.com/colormagazine/docs/color_ed_27_lr.

62 Iacoboni, M. (2016) The Mirror Neuron Revolution: Explaining What Makes Humans Social. *Scientific American*. Retrieved from https://www.scientificamerican.com/article/the-mirror-neuron-revolut/.

63 Child Development, *Ibid.*

64 Stanford University Medical Center. (2014, November 4). Oxytocin levels in blood, cerebrospinal fluid are linked, study finds. *ScienceDaily*. Retrieved from http:// www.sciencedaily.com/releases/2014/11/141104163013.htm.

65 Association for Psychological Science. (2007, September 26). Why Few People Are Devoid Of Racial Bias. *ScienceDaily*. Retrieved March 26, 2016 from www.sciencedaily.com/releases/2007/09/070924122814.htm.

66 Princeton University. (2011, June 6). The science of storytelling. *Psychology Today*. Retrieved from https://www.psychologytoday.com/blog/you-illuminated/201106/why-sharing-stories-brings-people-together

67 Aronson, J. (2004, November). The Threat of Stereotype. Educational Leadership: Closing Achievement Gaps. *ASCD*. Retrieved

from http://www.ascd.org/publications/educational-leadership/nov04/vol62/num03/toc.aspx.

68 Aronson. *Ibid.*

69 Northside Achievement Zone, Minneapolis, MN. http://northside-achievement.org/

CHAPTER THREE. S.A.V.E. Communications: Outsmarting the Defensive Brain

70 Hallowell, E., MD (2007). *CrazyBusy: Overstretched, Overbooked, and About to Snap! Strategies for Handling Your Fast-Paced Life.* New York, New York: Ballantine Books.

71 Burton, R., MD (2008). *On Being Certain: Believing You Are Right Even When You're Not.* New York, New York: St. Martin's Press.

72 Siegel, D., MD (2009). *Mindsight: The New Science of Personal Transformation.* New York, New York: Bantam.

73 Feusner, J., A Problem of perception? What research tells us about BDD. *International OCD Foundation.* Retrieved From https://bdd.iocdf.org/expert-opinions/problem-of-perception/

74 Iacoboni. *Ibid.*

75 Kosfeld M., Heinrichs M. (2005, June 2). Oxytocin increases trust in humans. *NCBI Resources.* Retrieved from https://www.ncbi.nlm.nih.gov/pubmed/15931222

76 Hallowell, E. (2008, February 21). Overloaded circuits: why smart people under perform. *Harvard Business Review Online.* Retrieved From https:www.harvardbusinessonline.hbspharvard.edu/hbsp/hbr/articles,

77   Pillay, S. (2016, February 29). Neuroscience can help you live a healthier life. Harvard Health Blog. Retrieved from http://www.health.harvard.edu/blog/neuroscience-can-help-you-live-a-healthier-life-201602299210

78   Hotz, R. L. (2009, June 19). A wandering mind heads straight towards insight: Researchers map the anatomy of the brain's breakthrough moments and reveal the payoff of daydreaming. *Wall Street Journal*. Retrieved from http://www.wsj.com/articles/SB124535297048828601.

79   Drexel University. (2016, March 7). Trust your aha! moments: Experiments show they're probably right. *ScienceDaily*. Retrieved June 27, 2016 from www.sciencedaily.com/releases/2016/03/160307144013.htm

80   Drexel University. *Ibid.*

81   Yuhas, D. (2014, October 2). Curiosity prepares the brain for better earning. *Scientific American Mind*. Retrieved from https://www.scientificamerican.com/article/curiosity-prepares-the-brain-for-better-learning/

82   University of California, Los Angeles. (2016) *Trivia Pamphlet*. Retrieved from http://www.loni.usc.edu/about_loni/education/brainTriviaBrochure.pdf

83   Shelia, H. and Stone, D. (2015). *Thanks for the Feedback: The Science and Art of Receiving Feedback Well*. Penguin Books, New York, New York.

84   Hotz, R. L. *Ibid*

CHAPTER FOUR. Choosing Inclusion: In the Moment Awareness

85   Hammerness, P. & Moore, M. (2012, January 18). Train your brain to focus. *Harvard Business Review*. Retrieved from https://hbr.org/2012/01/train-your-brain-to-focus

86 Tjan, A. (2012, July 19,) How leaders become self-aware.
    Harvard Business Review. Retrieved from https://hbr.org/2012/01/
    train-your-brain-to-focus

87 Kohler, L. (1962, May). Experiments with goggles. *Scientific American.*
    Retrieved from https://www.scientificamerican.com/article/
    experiments-with-goggles/

88 Ramachandran, V. (2007, January 8). The neurobiology of self-aware-
    ness. *The Edge.* Retrieved from https://www.edge.org/conversation/
    the-neurology-of-self-awareness

89 Davidson, R. Discovering ourselves: The science of emotion:
    Executive summary. *LCNMIH Decade of the Brain Home Page*
    Retrieved from http://www.loc.gov/loc/brain/emotion/Davidson.
    html

CHAPTER FIVE. Building the Larger Circle of We

90 Singer, T. (2013 June 24). Feeling others' pain: Transforming empa-
    thy into compassion. *Cognitive Neuroscience Society.* Retrieved from
    https://www.cogneurosociety.org/empathy_pain/

91 Association for Psychological Science. (2011, July 7). Teaching the
    neurons to meditate. *ScienceDaily.* Retrieved from http:// www.
    sciencedaily.com /releases/2011/07/110707173321.htm

92 Harvard Business School. (2011). Collaborating across cultures:
    Cultural metacognition & affect-based trust in creative collabora-
    tion. Retrieved from http://www.hbs.edu/faculty/Publication%20
    Files/11-127.pdf

93 University of California - Berkeley. (2016). What is mindfulness?
    Greater Good in Action. Retrieved from http://greatergood.berkeley.
    edu/topic/mindfulness/definition

94 University of California - Berkeley. *Ibid.*

95 University of Wisconsin - Madison. (2015, April 24). Mindfulness meditation reduces implicit age and race bias: The role of reduced automaticity of responding. *ResearchGate.* Retrieved fromhttps://www.researchgate.net/publication/269700255_Mindfulness_Meditation_Reduces_Implicit_Age_and_Race_Bias

96 Gendlin, E.(1981) *Focusing,* New York, New York: Bantam Dell

97 Amaral, J. & Oliveira, J. (2015). Limbic system: The center of emotions. The Healing Center On-Line. Retrieved from http://www.healing-arts.org/n-r-limbic.htm

98 Sousa, D. (2012). Brainwork: The Neuroscience Behind How We Lead Others. Bloomington, IN: Triple Nickel Press

99 Amir, O. (2008, July 22). Decisions tires your mind. Scientific American. Retrieved from https://www.scientificamerican.com/article/tough-choices-how-making/

100 Killgore, W. (2017, January 4). Effects of sleep deprivation on cognition. ResearchGate. Retrieved from https://www.researchgate.net/publication/47790667_Effects_of_sleep_deprivation_on_cognition

101 Godman, H. (2014, April 9). Regular exercise changes the brain to improve memory, thinking skills. *Harvard Health Blog.* Retrieved from http://www.health.harvard.edu/blog/regular-exercise-changes-brain-improve-memory-thinking-skills-201404097110

102 Childre, D. (2002) The inside story: Understanding the power of feelings. HeartMath Institute Booklet. Retrieved from https://www.heartmath.org/assets/uploads/2015/01/inside-story.pdf

103 Singer, T. *Ibid.*

104 Pillay, S. (2011) Your Brain and Business: The Neuroscience of Great Leaders. Upper Saddle River, New Jersey: Pearson Education

105 University of Wisconsin-Madison. (2007, June 25). Scans show meditation changes minds, increases attention. News. Retrieved from http://news.wisc.edu/brain-scans-show-meditation-changes-minds-increases-attention/

106 Laguipo, A. (2015, November 23). 7 Minutes of meditation can reduce racial prejudice: Study. TechTimes. Retrieved from http://www.techtimes.com/articles/109251/20151123/7-minutes-of-meditation-can-reduce-racial-prejudice-study.htm

107 The Energy Project: White Paper (2011). The X factor in engagement, productivity & performance. Retrieved from https://damonht.files.wordpress.com/2013/02/tep-whitepaper-2011.pdf

108 Willis, J. (2011, October 5). Three brain-based teaching strategies to build executive function in students. *Edutopia*. Retrieved from https://www.edutopia.org/blog/brain-based-teaching-strategies-judy-willis

109 Ritchtel, M. (2010, August 15). Your brain on computers. Outdoors and out of reach. *New York Times*. Retrieved from http://topics.nytimes.com/top/features/timestopics/series/your_brain_on_computers/index.html

110 Marsh, A., Henry, H., Pine, D. & Blair, R. (2010, February). Oxytocin improves specific recognition of positive facial expressions. ResearchGate. Retrieved from https://www.researchgate.net/publication/41579082_Oxytocin_improves_specific_recognition_of_positive_facial_expressions

111 Langer, E. J. Ibid.

112 University of California - Berkeley. Implicit and explicit memory and learning. Retrieved fromhttp://socrates.berkeley.edu/~kihlstrm/landMLandM.htm

113 Doidge, N. Ibid.

114 Pettigrew, T.F., Tropp L.R.,.& Pettigrew, T.F. (2006 May, 9). A meta-analytic test of intergroup contact theory. NCBI Resources. Retrieved from https://www.ncbi.nlm.nih.gov/pubmed/16737372

115 Martin, J., (2010, May 25). What the dalai lama learned from thomas merton. American Magazine. Retrieved from http://www.americamagazine.org/content/all-things/what-dalai-lama-learned-thomas-merton

Bibliography

Acoustical Society of America. (2014, October 29). The science of
    charismatic voices: How one man was viewed as authoritarian, then
    benevolent. *ScienceDaily*. Retrieved from http://www.sciencedaily.
    com/releases/2014/10/141029203947.htm.

American Psychological Association. (2011, September 1). Perception of
    facial expressions differ across cultures. *ScienceDaily*. Retrieved from
    http://www.sciencedaily.com/releases/2011/09/110901105510.htm.

Association for Psychological Science. (2010, August 3). Culture
    wires the brain: A cognitive neuroscience perspective.
    ScienceDaily. Retrieved from http://www.sciencedaily.com/releas-
    es/2010/08/100803113150.htm.

Association for Psychological Science. (2010, August 25). Oxytocin
    makes people trusting, but not gullible, study suggests. *ScienceDaily*.
    Retrieved May 17, 2012, from http://www.sciencedaily.com/releas-
    es/2010/08/100824103535.htm.

Association for Psychological Science. (2010, July 21). Getting an-
    gry can help negotiations in some cultures, hurt in others.
    ScienceDaily. Retrieved from http:/www.sciencedaily.com/releas-
    es/2010/07/100720123631.htm.

Association for Psychological Science. (2011, July 10). Teaching the neurons to mediate. *ScienceDaily*. Retrieved from http://www.sciencedaily.com/releases/2011/07/110707173321.htm.

Association for Psychological Science. (2011, January 4). Trust your gut...but only sometimes. *ScienceDaily*. Retrieved from http:/www.sciencedaily.com/releases/2011/01/110104114307.htm.

Association for Psychological Science. (2011, November 8). Which way you lean - physically - affects your decision making. *ScienceDaily*. Retrieved from http://www.sciencedaily.com/releases/2011/11/111108133053.htm.

Association for Psychological Science. (2012, January 27). The amygdala and fear are not the same thing. *ScienceDaily*. Retrieved from http://www.sciencedaily.com/releases/2012/01/120127162755.htm.

Association for Psychological Science. (2013, August 22). Engaging in a brief cultural activity can reduce implicit prejudice. *ScienceDaily*. Retrieved from http://www.sciencedaily.com/releases/2013/08/130822105040.htm.

Association for Psychological Science. (2014, June 9). Distance from conflict may promote wiser reasoning. *ScienceDaily*. Retrieved from http://www.sciencedaily.com/releases/2014/06/140609113349.htm.

Association for Psychological Science. (2014, September 8). Faces are more likely to seem alive when we want to feel connected. *ScienceDaily*. Retrieved from http://www.sciencedaily.com/releases/2014/09/140908135421.htm.

Association for Psychological Science. (2014, November 24). The sound of status: People know high-power voices when they hear them. Retrieved from http://www.sciencedaily.com/releases/2014/141124081040.htm.

Association for Psychological Science. (2015, January 7). Expressing anger linked with better health in some cultures. *ScienceDaily*. Retrieved from http://www.sciencedaily.com/releases/2015/01/150107122916.htm.

Association for Psychological Sciences. (2011, October 31). Don't worry, be happy: Understanding mindfulness meditation. *ScienceDaily*. Retrieved from http://www.sciencedaily.com/releases/2011/10/111031154134.htm.

Azar, B. (2010). Your brain on culture: The burgeoning field of cultural neuroscience is finding that culture influences brain development, and perhaps vice versa. *Monitor on Psychology*. Retrieved from http://www.apa.org/monitor/2010/11/neuroscience.aspx.

Bargh, J. (2014, January). How unconscious thought and perception affect our every waking moment: Unconscious impulses and desires impel what we think and do in ways Freud never dreamed of. *Scientific American*, pp. 23-37. Retrieved from http://www.scientificamerican.com/article/how-unconscious-thought-and-perception-affect-our-every-waking-moment/.

Barrett, L., Lindquist, K., & Gendron, M. (2011, October 3). In reading facial expressions, context is everything. *ScienceDaily*. Retrieved from http://www.sciencedaily.com/releases/2011/10/111003180438.htm.

Barsh, J., Cranston, S., & Craske, R. (2008). Centered leadership: How talented women thrive. *The Mckinsey Quarterly*.(4). Retrieved from http://www.mckinsey.com/global-themes/leadership/centered-leadership-how-talented-women-thrive.

Behar, A. (2005, Fall). An interview with Joshua Aronson: Distinguished NYU professor discusses his research (on stereotype threat). *Access, 11*(2). Retrieved from http://www.avid.org/dl/abo_access/access_ip_2005_joshuaaronson.pdf.

Berlin, H. (2011). The neural basis of the dynamic unconscious. *Neuropsychoanalysis, 13*, pp. 5-31. Retrieved from http://www.nyu.edu/gsas/dept/philo/faculty/block/papers/BerlinTreatment.pdf.

Bielefeld University. (2014, October 17). How the brain leads us to believe we have sharp vision. *ScienceDaily*. Retrieved from http://www.sciencedaily.com/releases/2014/10/141017101339.htm.

BioMed Central. (2009, September 16). Doctors' 'gut feelings" defined. Science Daily. Retrieved from http://www.sciencedaily.com/releases/2009/09/090916223738.htm.

Birshan, M., & Kar, J. (2012, July). Becoming more strategic: Three tips for any executive. *Strategy Practice*. Retrieved from http://www.mckinsey.com/business-functions/strategy-and-corporate-finance/our-insights/becoming-more-strategic-three-tips-for-any-executive.

Blackman, A. (2014, April 27). The inner workings of the executive brain: New research shows the best business minds make decisions differently than we thought. *The Wall Street Journal*. Retrieved from http://www.wsj.com/articles/the-inner-workings-of-the-executive-brain-1398388537.

Blanchard, K. (2013, August 10). Power robs the brain of empathy. *Science*. Retrieved from http://www.digitaljournal.com/article/356229.

Boeree, C. G. (2002). The Emotional Nervous System. Retrieved from http://www.slideshare.net/KrycesTorcato/general-psychology-part-1-written-by-d.

Boyatzis, R. (2011, January/February). Neuroscience and leadership: The promise of insights. *Ivey Business Journal*. Retrieved from http://iveybusinessjournal.com/publication/neuroscience-and-leadership-the-promise-of-insights/.

British Psychological Society. (2015, January 7). Staying in touch during out-of-office hours damages workers' wellbeing. *ScienceDaily*. Retrieved from http://www.sciencedaily.com/releases/2015/01/150107204557.htm.

British Psychological Society. (2012, October 26). How the negative trumps the positive in politics. *ScienceDaily*. Retrieved from http://www.sciencedaily.com/releases/2012/10/121026084643.htm.

British Psychological Society. (2014, December 4). What really helps women achieve a better work-life balance? Retrieved from http://www.sciencedaily.com/releases/2014/12/141204074150.htm.

British Psychological Society. (2015, January 7). University or university of life? Neither provides workers with necessary people skills. *ScienceDaily*. Retrieved from http://www.sciencedaily.com/releases/2015/01/150107204603.htm.

Buch, K. (2010, May 14). Brain break: Understanding the influence of brain functions on organizational effectiveness. *T & D Magazine*. Retrieved from http://www.td.org/Publications/Magazines/TD/TD-Archive/2010/05/Brain-Break-Understanding-the-Influence-of-Brain-Functions-on-Organizational-Effectiveness.

California Institute of Technology. (2011, September 29). Neuroscientists record novel responses to faces from single neurons in humans. *ScienceDaily*. Retrieved from http://www.sciencedaily.com/releases/2011/09/110929122753.htm.

Canton, N. (2012, September 28). Cell phone culture: How cultural differences affect mobile use. *CNN*. Retrieved from http://www.cnn.com/2012/09/27/tech/mobile-culture-usage/.

Carmeli, A., & Speitzer, G. M. (2009). Trust, connectivity, and thriving: Implications for innovative work behavior. *Journal of Creative Behavior, 3*, pp. 169-191.

Carmeli, A., Dutton, J. E., & Hardin, A. E. (n.d.). Respect as an engine for new ideas: Linking respectful engagement, relational information processing and creativity among employees and their teams. *Center for Positive Organizations*. Retrieved from http://positiveorgs.bus. umich.edu/articles/respect-as-an-engine-for-new-ideas-linking-respectful-engagment-relational-information-processing-and-creativity-among-employees-and-teams.

Carriero, R. (2012). The Kadesh peace treaty: World's oldest peace treaty. *Time Out Istanbul*. Retrieved from Voices: http://www.richcarriero.com/pdf/Kadesh.pdf.

Case Western Reserve University. (2014, March 24). Leaders wired to be task-focused or team-builders, but can be both. *ScienceDaily*. Retrieved from http://www.sciencedaily.com/releases/2014/03/140324104522.htm.

Cell Press. (2009, August 16). Facial expressions show language barriers, too. *ScienceDaily*. Retrieved from http://www.sciencedaily.com/releases/2009/08/090813142131.htm.

Cell Press. (2012, July 12). Individual differences in altruism explained by brain region involved in empathy. *ScienceDaily*. Retrieved from http://www.sciencedaily.com/releases/2012/07/120711123001.htm.

Cell Press. (2014, October 2). How curiosity changes the brain to enhance learning. *ScienceDaily*. Retrieved from http://www.sciencedaily.com/releases/2014/10/14/141002123631.htm.

Cell Press. (2014, October 14). Impressions shaped by facial appearance foster biased decisions. *ScienceDaily*. Retrieved from http://www.sciencedaily.com/releases/2014/10/141021135012.htm.

Cell Press. (2014, October 29). Liberal or conservative? Reactions to disgust are a dead giveaway. *ScienceDaily*. Retrieved from http://www.sciencedaily.com/releases/2014/10/141029124502.htm.

Concordia University. (2014, September 30). How to predict who will suffer the most from stress. *ScienceDaily*. Retrieved from http://www.sciencedaily.com/releases/2014/09/140930132724.htm.

Cooper, B. (2014, January 13). Why positive encouragement works better than criticism, according to science [Blog post]. *BufferSocial*. Retrieved from http://blog.bufferapp.com/why-positive-encourage-ment-works-better-than-criticism-according-to-science.

Cornell University. (2014, November 4). This just in: Political correct-ness pumps up productivity on the job. *ScienceDaily*. Retrieved from http://www.sciencedaily.com/releases/2014/11/141104183610.htm.

Cornell University. (2014, July 9). Study cracks how brain processes emotions. *ScienceDaily*. Retrieved from http://www.sciencedaily.com/releases/2014/07/140709135836.htm.

Cross cultural: Who's the boss? Americans respond faster to those with high social status. (2011, February 17). *ScienceDaily*. Retrieved from http://www.sciencedaily.com/releases/2011/02/110216185400.htm.

Crowley, M. (2015, February 5). Why engagement happens in employees' hearts, not their minds: Winning your employ-ees over to stick with the company long term involves an array of factors - but first among those is love. *Leadership*. Retrieved from http://www.fastcompany.com/3041948/why-engagement-happens-in-employeess-hearts-not-their-minds.

Davidson, R., & Begley, S. (February/March, 2012). The new science of feelings. *Newsweek*, pp. 46-51.

Deloitte Consulting. (2009). Why change now? Preparing for the work-place of tomorrow. Retrieved from http://www.federalnewsradio.com/wp-content/uploads/pdfs/WorkplaceofTomorrowFederal0721.pdf.

Desvaux, G., Devillard, S., & Sancier-Sultan, S. (2010, October). Women at the top of corporations: making it happen. *Women Matter 2010.* McKinsey & Company. Retrieved from http://www. mckinsey.com/business-functions/organization/our-insights/ women-at-the-top-of-corporations-making-it-happen.

FECYT - Spanish Foundation for Science and Technology. (2010, April 11). Empathy and violence have similar circuits in the brain, research suggests. *ScienceDaily.* Retrieved from http://www.science-daily.com/releases/2010/04/100409093405.htm.

Fredrickson, B. L. (n.d.). Leading with Positive Emotions. *Center for Positive Organizations.* Retrieved from http://www.bus.umich.edu/ FacultyResearch/Research/TryingTimes/PositiveEmotions.htm.

Frenkel, K. A. (2008, April 1). Even better than a personal best: When showing up a peer is more satisfying than succeeding alone. *Scientific American.* Retrieved from http://www.scientificamerican. com/article/even-better-than-a-personal-best/.

Gallup Consulting. (2009). The next discipline: applying behavioral economics to drive growth and profitability. Retrieved from http:// www.gallup.com/services/178028/next-discipline-pdf.aspx.

Garland, E. L., Fredrickson, B., Kring, A. M., Johnson, D. P., Meyer, P. S., & Penn, D. L. (2010). Upward spirals of positive emotions counter downward spirals of negativity: Insights from the broaden-and-build theory and affective neuroscience on the treatment of emotion dysfunctions and deficits in psychopathology. *Clinical Science Review.* Retrieved from http://www.sciencedirect.com/science/article/pii/ S0272735810000425.

Gelatt, H. (1989). Positive uncertainty: A new decision-making frame-work for counseling. *Journal of Counseling Psychology, 36,* pp. 252-256. Retrieved from http://depts.washington.edu/apac/round-table/10-23-06_positive_uncertainty.pdf.

George, W., Sims, P., McLean, A., & Mayer, D. (2007, February).
Discovering your authentic leadership. *Harvard
Business Review*. Retrieved from http://hbr.org/2007/02/
discovering-your-authentic-leadership.

Gerstandt, J. (n.d.). Considering the intersection of inclusion and talent:
Being competitive for talent means being serious about inclusion.
Future of Talent Institute. Retrieved from http://www.joegerstandt.
com/downloads/JoeGerstandt-InclusionAndTalent.pdf.

Gibson, J. (2013, January 26 26). Joy to the world: Empathy and positive emotions. *Brain Blogger*. Retrieved from http://brainblogger.
com/2013/01/26/joy-to-the-world-empathy-and-positive-emotions/.

Gladding, R. (2011, June 21). Don't believe everything you think or feel:
Ending unhelpful overanalyzing and breaking free from emotional
reasoning. *Psychology Today*. Retrieved from http://www.psycholo-
gytoday.com/blog/use-your-mind-change-your-brain/201106/
don-t-believe-everything-you-think-or-feel.

Gollwitzer, P. (1999, July). Implementation intentions: Strong effects of
simple plans. *American Psychologist., 54*(7), pp. 493-503.

Gorman, J. (2014, January 6). The brain, in exquisite detail. *The New
York Times*. Retrieved January 9, 2014, from http://www.nytimes.
com/2014/01/07/science/the-brain-in-exquisite-detail.html?_r=0.

Gowin, J. (2012, June 28). How lack of insight sustains addiction.
Psychology Today. Retrieved from https://www.psychologytoday.com/
blog/you-illuminated/201206/how-lack-insight-sustains-addiction.

Graham, L. (2013). *Bouncing Back: Rewiring Your Brain for Maximum
Resilience and Well-Being*. Novato

California. New Library Press.

Guynn, J. (2015, August 7). #ILookLikeAnEngineer hashtag
may get its own ad campaign. *USA Today*. Retrieved
from http://www.usatoday.com/story/tech/2015/08/06/
viral-ilooklikeanengineer-hashtag-advertising-campaign/31249317/.

Habermacher, A. (2011, November/December). No head for decision
making? The neuroscience of distorted decisions and how to avoid
them. pp. 52-55.

Hallowell, E. (2005, January). Overloaded circuits: why smart people
underperform. *Harvard Business Review*. Retrieved March 30, 2012

Hardman., H. (2006, September 25). How the brain controls emotions.
Medical News Today. Retrieved from http://www.medicalnewstoday.
com/releases/52415.php.

HeartMath LLC. (2002). *HeartMath Institute - Expanding Heart
Connections*. Retrieved from The Inside Story - Understanding
the Power of Feelings.: http://www.heartmath.org/resources/
downloads/the-inside-story/.

Holloway, K. (2015, March 2). Hey, smug white people: you (yes, you are
a racist, too. Retrieved March 3, 2015

Hopkins, A. (2006, February 23). Emotionally attached: The role of feelings in decision making. *Serendip*. Retrieved from http://serendip.
brynmawr.edu/bb/neuro/neuro06/web1/ahopkins.html.

Hotz, R. L. (2009, June 19). A wandering mind heads straight towards insight: Researchers map the anatomy of the brain's
breakthrough moments and reveal the payoff of daydreaming.
Wall Street Journal. Retrieved from http://www.wsj.com/articles/
SB124535297048828601.

Human Factors and Ergonomics Society. (2014, July 2014). Say 'no' to interruptions, 'yes' to better work. *ScienceDaily*. Retrieved from http://
www.sciencedaily.com/releases/2014/07/140714122606.htm.

IDIBELL-Bellvitge Biomedical Research Institute. (2014, November 5). Brain dissociates emotional response from explicit memory in fearful situations. *ScienceDaily*. Retrieved from http://www.sciencedaily.com/releases/2014/11/141105112618.htm.

Instituto D'Or de Pesquisa e Ensino. (2014, May 21). Training brain patterns of empathy using functional brain imaging. *ScienceDaily*. Retrieved from http://www.sciencedaily.com/releases/2014/05/140521180016.htm.

Karolinska Institutet. (2014, September 25). How physical exercise protects the brain from stress-induced depression. *ScienceDaily*. Retrieved from http://www.sciencedaily.com/releases/2014/09/140925131345.htm.

Kluger, J. (2015, June 2015). Why you're pretty much unconscious all the time. *Time Magazine*. Retrieved from http://swiffypreviews.googleusercontent.com/view/o/b5ecff6a-6533-4f7a-b0e3-22c7bec487f0/300x600_Deadline_HTML5.html.

Lee, C. (2009, October 15). *Angioma Alliance*. Retrieved from Cognitive Rehabilitation: http://www.angioalliance.org/pages/aspx?content=83.

Legault, L., & Inzlicht, M. (2013). Self-determination, self-regulation, and the brain: autonomy improves performance by enhancing neuroaffective responsiveness to self-regulation failure. *Journal of Personality and Social Psychology, 105*(1).

Lende, D. (2010, November 26). Cultural neuroscience - Culture and the brain [Web log]. *Plos Blogs*. Retrieved from http://blogs.plos.org/neuroanthropology/2010/11/26/cultural-neuroscience-%E2%80%93-culture-and-the-brain/.

Levitin, D. J. (2014, August 9). Hit the reset button in your brain. *New York Times*. Retrieved from http://nyti.ms/1pl8y19.

Lieberman, D. M. (n.d.). Is racism the neural adversary of the social mind? *The Social Brain.*

Livermore, D. (2014, September 15). I get it. I'm biased. So now what? *Cultural Intelligence Center.* Retrieved from http://culturalq. com/i-get-it-im-biased-so-now-what/.

LTP - Make a Memory. (n.d.). Retrieved from Genes to Cognition Online: http://www.g2conline.org.

Lund University. (2015, December 4). Rudeness at work is contagious, study shows. *ScienceDaily.* Retrieved from http://www.sciencedaily. com/releases/2015/12/151204094352.htm.

Massachusetts General Hospital. (2012, November 12). Meditation appears to produce enduring changes in emotional processing of the brain. *ScienceDaily.* Retrieved from http://www.sciencedaily.com/ releases/2012/11/121112150339.htm.

Massachusetts Institute of Technology. (2014, June 12). Synchronized brain waves enable rapid learning. *ScienceDaily.* Retrieved from http://www.sciencedaily.com/releases/2014/06/140614061212121354. htm.

Massachusetts Institute of Technology. (2014, June 12). When good people do bad things: Being in a group makes some people lose touch with their personal moral beliefs. *ScienceDaily.* Retrieved from http://www.sciencedaily.com/releases/2014/06/140612104950.htm.

Massachusetts Institute of Technology. (2014, October 6). Workplace diversity can help bottom line, study shows. *ScienceDaily.* Retrieved from http://www.sciencedaily.com/releases/2014/10/141006114053. htm.

Massachusetts General Hospital. (2012, June 24). Brain structure helps guide behavior by anticipating changing demands.

ScienceDaily. Retrieved from http://sciencedaily.com/releases/2012/06/120624134949.htm.

Matthews, C. (2014, September 2). He dropped one letter in his name while applying for jobs, and the responses rolled in. *The Huffington Post*. Retrieved from http://www.huffingtonpost.com/2014/09/02/jose-joe-job-discrimination_n_5753880.html.

McFarland, W. (2012, October 2016). This is your brain on organizational change. *Harvard Business Review*. Retrieved from http://hbr.org/2012/10/this-is-your-brain-on-organizational-change.

Meyer, M. (2009, October 10). How culture shaped our mind and brain. *Brain Blogger*. Retrieved from http://brainblogger.com/2009/10/10/how-culture-shapes-our-mind-and-brain/.

Michigan State University. (2011, October 20). I vs. we: Individuals perform better when focused on team's effort. *ScienceDaily*. Retrieved from http://www.sciencedaily.com/releases/2011/10/111020122323.htm.

Michigan State University. (2012, July 30). When rules change, brain falters. *ScienceDaily*. Retrieved from http://www.sciencedaily.com/releases/2012/07/120730124239.htm.

Morgan, N. (2015, June 30). Why conscious thought is mostly an illusion and what that means for public speakers. *Forbes*. Retrieved from http://www.forbes.com/sites/nickmorgan/2015/06/30/why-conscious-thought-is-mostly-an-illusion-and-what-that-means-for-public-speakers/#1dc89ec6ae736de2fb7ae731.

Murray, E. A. (2007, November 11). The amygdala, reward and emotion. *Trends in Cognitive Science.*, 11(11). Retrieved from http://www.ncbi.nlm.nih.gov/pubmed/17988930.

Naqvi, N., Shiv, B., & Bechara, A. (2006). The role of emotion in decision making: A cognitive neuroscience perspective. *Current Directions in Psychological Science, 15*(5), pp. 260-264.

National Institute for Physiological Sciences. (2012, November 9). Scientific explanation to why people perform better after receiving a compliment. *ScienceDaily.* Retrieved from http://www.sciencedaily.com/releases//2012/11/121109111517.htm.

National Institutes of Health. (2015, August). Connection between positive feelings and openness to ideas. *NIH News in Health.* Retrieved from http://newsinhealth.nih.gov/issues/aug2015.

New York University. (2013, January 10). Researchers find causality in the eye of the beholder. *ScienceDaily.* Retrieved from http:/www.sciencedaily.com/releases/2013/01/130110121028.htm.

New York University. (2014, August 2014). Our brains judge a face's trustworthiness, even when we can't see it. *ScienceDaily.* Retrieved from http://www.sciencedaily.com/releases/2014/08/140805220718.htm.

Nodjimbadem, K. (2015, September 2015). 'Hidden Brain' podcast will make you think twice about your unconscious mind. *Smithsonian Magazine.* Retrieved from http://www.smithsonianmag.com/science-nature/hidden-brain-podcast-will-make-you-think-twice-about-your-unconscious-mind-180956521.

North Carolina State University. (2014, December 9). Online students give instructors higher marks if they think instructors are men. *ScienceDaily.* Retrieved from http://www.sciencedaily.com/releases/2014/12/141209120137.htm.

NPSC. (2006, July). What Matters to Student Success: A Review of the Literature. *National Center for*

Education Statistics. Retrieved from https://nces.ed.gov/npec/pdf/kuh_
    team_report.pdf.

Ohio State University. (2012, January 19). When it comes to accept-
    ing evolution, gut feelings trump facts. *ScienceDaily*. Retrieved from
    http:///www.sciencedaily.com/releases/2012/01/120119133926.htm.

Parry, L. (2015, November 19). Is meditation the key to combating rac-
    ism? Seven minutes of loving-kindness contemplation 'reduces racial
    bias.'. *DAILYMAIL.COM*. Retrieved from http://www.dailymail.co.uk/
    health/article-3325998/Is-MEDITATION-key-combating-racism-
    Seven-minutes-loving-kindness-contemplation-reduces-racial-bias.
    html#ixzz3zg7et9UP.

Pillay, S. (2014, February 20). What to do when you can't control
    your stress. *Harvard Business Review*. Retrieved from http://hbr.
    org/2014/02/what-to-do-when-you-cant-control-your-stress?utm_
    medium=referral.

PLOS. (2014, September 18). Pupil size shows reliability of decisions,
    before information on decision is presented. Retrieved from http://
    www.sciencedaily.com/releases/2014/09/140918141546.htm.

Powell, D. (2013, March 1). Create a 'toward' state: Author Rock applies
    brain research to change management. *NIH Record*. Retrieved from
    http://nihrecord.nih.gov/newsletters/2013/03_01_2013/story3.htm.

Prehn, A. (2012). Create reframing mindsets through Framestorm. *Neuro
    Leadership Journal*(4).

Public Library of Science. (2012, December 5). Hearing positive verbs can
    induce unconscious physical response. *ScienceDaily*. Retrieved from
    http://www.sciencedaily.com/releases/2012/12/121205200055.htm.

Rock, D. (2009). Managing with the brain in mind. *Strategy and Business
    Magazine*(56). Retrieved from http://www.strategy-business.com/
    article/09306?gko=5df7f.

Rockstuhl, T., Hong, D., Ng, D., Ang, D., & Chiu, D. (2010). The culturally intelligent brain: From detecting to bridging cultural differences. *Neuro Leadership Journal.*(3). Retrieved from http://neuroleadership. com/portfolio-items/the-culturally-intelligent-brain-from-detecting-to-bridging-cultural-differences-vol-3/.

Ryan, J. (2011, August 12). What neuroscience can teach leaders: From brain science comes optimism. Ignore its power, and you'll deprive yourself and your workers of greater skills. *Bloomberg Businessweek.* Retrieved from http://www.bloomberg.com/news/ articles/2011-08-12/what-neuroscience-can-teach-leaders.

Sapolsky, R. (2013, July 28). Are humans hard-wired for racial prejudice? *Los Angeles Times.* Retrieved from http://articles.latimes.com/2013/ jul/28/opinion/la-oe-sapolsky-brain-and-race-20130728.

Sauter, D. A., Haun, D. B., & LeGuen, O. (2011, November 2). Understanding emotions without language. *ScienceDaily.* Retrieved from http://www.sciencedaily.com/releases/2011/11/111102093045. htm.

Sautoy, M. D. (n.d.). Brain scans can reveal your decisions 7 seconds before you 'decide'. Retrieved from http://exploringthemind.com/ the-mind/brain-scans-can-reveal-your-decisions-7-seconds-be-fore-you-decide.

Schmidt, M.V., & Schwabe, L. (2011, September/October). Splintered by stress: Psychological pressure can make you more attentive, improving your memory and ability to learn. But too much stress can have the opposite effect. *Scientific American Mind*, pp. 22-29. Retrieved from http://www.scientificamerican.com/article/ splintered-by-stress/.

Schwartz, Dr. J., & Rock, D. (2006, November). The neuroscience of leadership [Webinar]. Retrieved from http://webcasts.td.org/ webinar/213.

Schwartz, J., Gaito, P., & Lennick, D. (2011, February 22). 'That's the way we (used to) do things around here'. *Strategy and Business Magazine, 62.* Retrieved from http://www.strategy-business.com/article/11109?gko=8928a.

Scientific American Mind. (2008). Even better than a personal best: Why showing up a peer is more satisfying than succeeding alone. p. 17. Retrieved from http://www.scientificamerican.com/article/even-better-than-a-personal-best/.

Society for Personality and Social Psychology. (2014, October 24). Receiving gossip about others promotes self-reflection, growth. *ScienceDaily.* Retrieved from http://www.sciencedaily.com/releases/2014/10/141024082613.htm.

Society for Research in Child Development. (2011, September 12). Awareness of ethnicity-based stigma found to start early. *ScienceDaily.* Retrieved from http://www.sciencedaily.com/releases/2011/08/110830082046.htm.

Stanford University Medical Center. (2014, November 4). Oxytocin levels in blood, cerebrospinal fluid are linked, study finds. *ScienceDaily.* Retrieved from http://www.sciencedaily.com/releases/2014/11/141104163013.htm.

The Economist. (2012, December 8). Think yourself well. You can. But it helps to think well of yourself in the first place. Retrieved from http://www.economist.com/news/science-and-technology/21567876-you-can-it-helps-think-well-yourself-first-place-think-yourself.

The Energy Project. (2011). Energy: the X factor in engagement, productivity, & performance. *A White Paper by The Energy Project.* Retrieved from http://www.theenergyproject.com.

The Webb Patterson Report. (2005, Winter). Successes and failures in U.S. corporate diversity programs. Retrieved from http://www.webbpatterson.com.

Tufts University. (2011, September 26). Changing race by changing clothes? Stereotypes and status symbols impact if a face is viewed as black or white. *ScienceDaily*. Retrieved from http://www.science-daily.com/releases/2011/09/110926173121.htm.

University of Arizona. (2014, September 16). Don't underestimate your mind's eye: Objects don't need to be seen to impact decision-making. *ScienceDaily*. Retrieved from http://www.sciencedaily.com/releases/2014/09/140916142811.htm.

University of Exeter. (2014, November 7). Brain's response to threat silenced when we are reminded of being loved and cared for. *ScienceDaily*. Retrieved from http://www.sciencedaily.com/releas-es/2014/11/141107111025.htm.

Universitat Bonn. (2014, November 13). Oxytocin helps to better overcome fear. *ScienceDaily*. Retrieved from http://www.sciencedaily.com/releases/2014/11/141113110014.htm.

Universite de Montreal. (2014, August 20). Targeted brain training may help you multitask better. *ScienceDaily*. Retrieved from http://www.sciencedaily.com/releases/2014/08/140820091050.htm.

University of California - Berkeley. (2014, December 3). Brain net-work detected that gives humans superior reasoning skills. *ScienceDaily*. Retrieved from http://www.sciencedaily.com/releas-es/2014/12/141203142636.htm.

University of California - Los Angeles. (2007, July 23). Culture influences brain cells: Brain's mirror neurons swayed by ethnicity and culture. *ScienceDaily*. Retrieved from http://www.sciencedaily.com/releas-es/2007/07/070718002115.htm.

University of California - Los Angeles. (2011, October 3). How the brain makes memories: Rhythmically. *ScienceDaily*. Retrieved from http://www.sciencedaily.com/releases.2011/10/111003161935.htm.

University of California - Riverside. (2014, November 17). Ideas from middle managers are less likely to be passed to company leaders in organizations with more hierarchy. *ScienceDaily*. Retrieved from http://www.sciencedaily.com/releases/2014/11/141117130851.htm.

University of California - San Diego. (2009, April 7). Is there a seat of wisdom in the brain? *ScienceDaily*. Retrieved from http://www.sciencedaily.com/releases/2009/04/090406192244.htm.

University of California - Santa Barbara. (2013, March 26). Mindfulness improves reading ability, working memory, and task-focus. *ScienceDaily*. Retrieved from http://www.sciencedaily.com/releases/2013/03/130326133339.htm.

University of Chicago Booth School of Business. (2014, October 14). Uncertain reward more motivating than sure thing, study finds. *ScienceDaily*. Retrieved from http://www.sciencedaily.com/releases/2014/10/141014114750.htm.

University of Colorado Denver. (2015, January 8). Ethnic discrimination and health: Direct link found. *ScienceDaily*. Retrieved from http://www.sciencedaily.com/releases/2015/01/150108084907.htm.

University of Groningen. (2011, April 27). Music changes perception, research shows. *ScienceDaily*. Retrieved from http://www.sciencedaily.com/releases/2011/04/110427101606.htm.

University of Illinois at Urbana-Champaign. (2007, May 3). Culture sculpts neural response to visual stimuli, new research indicates. *ScienceDaily*. Retrieved from http://www.sciencedaily.com/releases/2007/05/070501115036.htm.

University of Kansas. (2015, January 7). Study finds partisanship most fierce among highly educated Americans. *ScienceDaily*. Retrieved from http://www.sciencedaily.com/releases/2015/01/150107151104.htm.

University of Kent. (2014, December 1). Athletes perform better when exposed to subliminal visual cues. *ScienceDaily*. Retrieved from http://www.sciencedaily.com/releases/2014/12/141201100423.htm.

University of Leicester. (2014, September 26). Neuroscientists use morphed images of Hollywood celebrities to reveal how neurons make up your mind. *ScienceDaily*. Retrieved from http://www.sciencedaily.com/releases/2014/09/140926112106.htm.

University of Pittsburgh Schools of the Health Sciences. (2016, January 4). Racial bias may be conveyed by doctors' body language. *ScienceDaily*. Retrieved from http://www.sciencedaily.com/releases/2016/01/160104130816.htm.

University of Southampton. (2015, January 6). Corporate philanthropy increases workers' productivity. *ScienceDaily*. Retrieved from http://www.sciencedaily.com/releases/2015/01/150106203000.htm.

University of Southern California Marshall School of Business. (2014, July 10). Energy of business leaders rises, but productivity declines. *ScienceDaily*. Retrieved from http://www.sciencedaily.com/releases/2014/07/140701030552.htm.

University of Toronto Scarborough. (2011, October 3). Fighting prejudice through imitation: Asking white people to mirror the movements of a black person lowers their levels of implicit prejudice. *ScienceDaily*. Retrieved from http://www.sciencedaily.com/releases/2011/10/111003132237.htm.

University of Utah. (2014, September 22). Firelight talk of the Kalahari Bushmen: Did tales told over fires aid our social and cultural evolution? *ScienceDaily*. Retrieved from http://www.sciencedaily.com/releases/12014/09/140922152809.htm.

University of Washington. (2014, May 19). Favoritism, not hostility, causes most discrimination. *ScienceDaily*. Retrieved from http://www.sciencedaily.com/releases/2014/05/140519060609.htm.

University of Washington. (n.d.). *Brain plasticity: What is it?* Retrieved from http://faculty.washington.edu/chudler/plast.html.

University of Waterloo. (2015, March 5). Reliance on smartphones linked to lazy thinking. *ScienceDaily*. Retrieved from http://www.sciencedaily.com/releases/2015/03/150305110546.htm.

University of Wisconsin - Madison. (2012, September 13). Stress breaks loops that hold short-term memory together. *ScienceDaily*. Retrieved from http://www.sciencedaily.com/releases/2012/09/120913173025.htm.

Uppsala University. (2012, September 20). Fear can be erased from brain, research shows. *ScienceDaily*. Retrieved from http://www.sciencedaily.com/releases/2012/09/120920141155.htm.

Virginia Tech. (2012, January 22). Group settings can diminish expressions of intelligence, especially among women. *ScienceDaily*. Retrieved from http://www.sciencedaily.com/releases/2012/01/120122201215.htm.

Washington State University. (2015, December 28). To bolster a new year's resolution, ask, don't tell: Study finds that questioning influences behavior. *ScienceDaily*. Retrieved from http://www.sciencedaily.com/releases/2015/12/151228124712.htm.

Waytz, A., & Mason, M. (2013, July/August). Your brain at work: What a new approach to neuroscience can teach us about management. *Harvard Business Review*, pp. 3-11. Retrieved from http://hbr.org/2013/07/your-brain-at-work.

Widrich, L. (n.d.). The science of storytelling: Why telling a story is the most powerful way to activate our brains. *Buffer*. Retrieved from https://blog.bufferapp.com/science-of-storytelling-why-telling-a-story-is-the-most-powerful-way-to-activate-our-brains.

Wikipedia. (n.d.). *Wikipedia*. Retrieved from Cross-race effect: https://en.wikipedia.org/wiki/Cross-race_effect.

Wolpert, S. (2008, July 9). Scientists learn how what you eat affects your brain - and those of your kids. *UCLA News*. Retrieved from http://newsroom.ucla.edu/releases/scientists-learn-how-food-affects-52668.

Yale University. (2008, April 4). People accept anger in men, but women who lose their temper are seen as less competent, study shows. *ScienceDaily*. Retrieved from http://www.sciencedaily.com-/releases/2008/04/0804022152707.htm.

Yale University. (2014, October 20). Positive subliminal messages on aging improve physical functioning in elderly. *ScienceDaily*. Retrieved from http://www.sciencedaily.com/releases/2014/10/141020145223.htm.

Zetlin, M. (2012, September 12). Listening to complainers is bad for your brain. *The Huffington Post*. Retrieved from http://www.huffingtonpost.com/2012/09/12/listening-to-complainers-_n_1877399.html.

About the Authors

Mary E. Casey, M.A.

Mary Casey, M.A., brings over 25 years' experience providing training and custom program design in the areas of diversity and inclusion, leadership development and teams building. Working with organizations such as Microsoft, General Mills, American Express, PepsiCo, Seagate and others, Mary brings exceptional skills in developing and facilitating. Mary has trained many other trainers, and been a lead facilitator in large scale including training initiatives that involved training 20,000 + employees. Mary's background also includes working in the UK for seven years as a senior consultant for Domino Perspectives providing leadership training in organizations throughout the UK and Europe.

Mary is Co-Founder of BrainSkills@Work - a consultancy that provides neuroscience-based training and coaching programs that provide individuals and organizations with new tools, strategies and skills for working *with the* brain to increase their effectiveness while staying resilient and open minded during these times of significant change and complexity.

In May 2012 Mary achieved advanced certification as a NeuroBusiness coach at Harvard with Dr. Srini Pillay (Harvard Medical School professor and CEO of NeuroBusiness Group). In 2012, Mary co-founded the Connemara Centre in Connemara, Ireland with colleague Geraldine Bown where they offer their renowned Authentic Women Leader Program - The Diamond Edge. Also with Geraldine Bown, Mary co-authored, From *Diversity to Unity: Creating the Energy of Connection,* published in 2002.

Mary's educational background includes a Master's Degree in Training and Organization Development from the University of Minnesota. Mary is also licensed to administer and facilitate: Situational Leadership, Myers Briggs Type Indicator, the DISC Personality Profile, Targeted Selection, and she is a certified HeartMath provider. Mary also holds a Master's Certificate from the NLP Institute in Group Leadership Dynamics. Mary is also a practicing yoga instructor and cares deeply about personal wellness and cultivating the body, mind, spirit connection.

Shannon Murphy Robinson, M.A.

Shannon Murphy Robinson, M.A., is a highly sought after organizational consultant, trainer and executive coach. She brings a wealth of experience in global diversity and inclusion, intercultural management, leadership development, and executive presentation skills. Shannon has over 20 years successfully creating and implementing large-scale diversity and inclusion training initiatives (20,000+ employees) with Fortune 500, for-profit and non-profit clients such as Deloitte, Deluxe, Be the Match, General Mills, GlaxoSmithKline, Champlain College, Boston Scientific, Mayo Clinic, Cargill, and others.

Shannon is Co-Founder of BrainSkills@Work™, a consulting firm that applies neuroscience and the latest brain research to developing leadership effectiveness, diversity and inclusion skills and cross-cultural competencies. In May, 2012 she achieved advanced certification as a NeuroBusiness Coach at Harvard with Dr. Srini Pillay (Harvard Medical School professor and CEO of NeuroBusiness Group). Shannon co-authored the neuroscience-based BrainStates Management™ Self-Assessment, and a white paper on "The Neuroscience of Inclusion: Managing Unconscious Bias."

Formerly a Vice President for ProGroup, a leader in providing diversity and inclusion programs globally, Shannon designed multi-year strategic global training initiatives, launched and managed affiliates across three continents, certified trainers, and lead many client engagement teams. With profit & loss and sales responsibility for 48% of the firm's revenues, Shannon knows exactly what she is talking about when she speaks to leaders. She knows what it is like to take a message and get it to translate across lines, across cultures, and ultimately, end with execution.

Shannon is on the faculty of the Intercultural Communication Institute in Portland, Oregon where she teaches workshops on the neuroscience of inclusion. She has a M.A. in Intercultural Communication, with an emphasis on leadership training and organizational development from American University, School of International Service, in Washington D.C.. She is certified in the Intercultural Development Inventory (IDI), Traditional Chinese Medicine and Quantum Healing. Her infectious style and warm candor have made her a favorite keynote speaker, presenter and trainer.

Printed in the USA
CPSIA information can be obtained
at www.ICGtesting.com
LVHW012306221223
767010LV00006B/210